CHOOSE FAITH AND GRACE

CHOOSE FAITH: RECEIVE FAITH and GOD'S LIVING WORD, GRACE!

RICHARD A. HARDIN

Amazon.com/Richard-A-Hardin/e/B09J2YHCVB

Choose Faith and Grace by Richard A. Hardin
ISBN: 1453664432 EAN-13: 9781453664438

Copyright # 2010, by Richard A Hardin. All Rights Reserved.
No part of this book may be reproduced, stored in a retrieval system, or transmitted in any way by any means, electronic, mechanical, photocopy, recording or otherwise without the prior permission of the author except as provided by the USA copyright law.

All scripture quotes are taken from the King James Version, Cambridge, 1769.

Dedication

This book is dedicated to the people in our society who have unfulfilled or empty hearts that only the Lord Jesus and our Heavenly Father can satisfy through their Living Word, Christ. Even though most people are presently seeking fulfillment through other means, (power, fame, money, drugs or sex), my prayer is that the message in this book will guide many to receiving God's Living Word, Christ, into their hearts. Christ is mankind's only solution to heart problems because God created us all alike in that only His Spirit can satisfy our hearts.

Thanks

I want to express my thanks to my son, Dwain Hardin, DNA Graphics, for the beautiful design and layout of my book and cover; also, my many thanks to Michael Grady, Rose University Adjunct English Professor, for his help with the commas, colons: and periods.

TABLE OF CONTENTS

INTRODUCTION 7
Christian Leaders are Ignorant of Biblical Faith and Grace 17

CHOOSE FAITH... 21
Doubt 26
Seeking 32
Belief Point 39
Unbelief 43
Doubt, Seeking, Belief Point, Unbelief 51
Faith 53
Doubt To Faith 61
Hope, Doubt, Seeking, Belief, Trust, Faith, and Walking-by-Faith 66
Jesus' Faith 74
Measure of Faith 79
All Men Have Not Faith 82
Not All People Are Children of God 83
Faith Does Not Come By Hearing, and Hearing, and Hearing! 84
God Respects His Word – Not People! 85

...AND GRACE 89

CONCLUSION 93
BOOKS BY THE AUTHOR 97
WEEKLY RADIO PROGRAM 97

INTRODUCTION

I am an Electrical Engineer, and in 1974, after thinking for 24 years that I was a Christian since age nine, I actually became a Christian. At that time I was a Captain in the United States Air Force and was assigned to the Memphis State University ROTC Detachment. My duties included representing USAF ROTC to high school advisors and assisting college ROTC units in the states of Arkansas, Mississippi and Shelby County, Tennessee which included Memphis. I spent most of my time traveling to visit high schools, colleges, and attending state counselor and teacher conventions where I would set up booths and pass out ROTC materials to those who were interested. With a wife, and four children below the age of ten and me being away from home so much, my family life began to crumble and led me to call out to God for help one night on my knees at my living room couch. I did not pray a very decent prayer; therefore, it was very fortunate that God has a lot of mercy and that I was sincere and meant it with all my heart. I basically said, "God, if you are real like the Bible says, and You want to have a personal relationship with me like it says You had with David, Moses, Paul and the other people of the Bible, then I am asking You to do that. I don't want any more of this religious mess with no answers, no help, no anything, just going through rituals. If You are real, please forgive me of my sins, for I know I have a lot of them, and show me You are real because if You are real like the Bible says You should be able to talk to me in a way that I will know it is You without any doubt. If You created me, then You could make me know some way that it is You talking to me. I am not going to stop drinking, smoking, cussing, or stop anything else, and I am not going to dress up and start carrying my Bible to church again, either, until I know it is You, in such a way that in six months or so from now no one can convince me that I just had

CHOOSE FAITH AND GRACE
INTRODUCTION

an emotional experience. I want to know You and if You are real! What I have had so far is worthless, so if You don't show me You are really real, then I am going to just forget this religious thing and go out with a blast. And, I am not going to just go on a good feeling either because there are good feelings all over town right now. So, I want to know You are real and that You want to have a relationship with me, and if so, then I will give You my life and try to serve You the best I can for the rest of my life, in Jesus name, Amen."

Now that I know how real God is, and I have quite a bit of fearful respect for God, I do not think I could ever recommend anyone approaching God with that type attitude or demanding nature. I am just so thankful that in His mercy, He heard the cry of a desperate heart and answered the cry by forgiving me and sending the Spirit of His Son Jesus Christ into my heart. He created in me a new heart and adopted me into His family as a joint heir with Jesus, and I became one of His children as stated in *Galatians 4:6-7, "And because ye are sons, God hath sent forth the Spirit of His Son into your hearts, crying, Abba, Father. (7) Wherefore thou are no more a servant, but a son; and if a son, then an heir of God through Christ."*

My life and heart changed so suddenly in May 1974 that I felt like I had been transplanted into a new world. I immediately lost my worship or "love" for both my new Lincoln Town Car, which I had special ordered from the factory with special pretty paint, leather interior, beautiful music system, and my fire-engine red, '57 Ford T-Bird, with a white clip-off top. A couple days after my prayer when my wife recommended that we should get family vehicles so the children would be more comfortable, I almost choked as I responded and realized I was speaking in agreement with her and really meant it from my heart. As I was saying the words of agreement to her, I realized that just a few days before I had "loved" those cars so much that the only way I would have gotten rid of them was to have them stolen, to have been paid about ten times what they were worth, or for me to have been shot. I was not just saying the words in

CHOOSE FAITH AND GRACE
INTRODUCTION

agreement to try to be nice; I knew in my heart that I really meant it. I also knew something drastic had happened inside me which I did not understand for me to have changed inside so fast that it almost seemed like overnight.

My life had been so messed up before my prayer that I had a few people in my life I was planning to try to harm. I was so messed up inside that when I thought of hurting them, I felt good, and one day as I was walking up to my house thinking that maybe I should not try to hurt them , I felt so bad that I said to myself, "Boy, you've really flipped." I thought about hurting them and felt good, then thought about not hurting them and felt bad. I at least remembered from all those years of going to church that I should have felt good trying to help others, not when I wanted to hurt them. I had been in neutral as far as approaching any of the people because I knew the hunter has the advantage in such situations. I could do what I wanted to do anytime I chose; I had the advantage. My prayer took place during the time I was waiting, and I was very busy for a few days after my prayer with my job, children and sick wife which kept my mind occupied and not thinking of the people I wanted to hurt. Then one day all of a sudden I thought of them, and I was shocked! At first I was confused about how I could have forgotten about them for so many days, and I was confused about the feelings that were going on inside of me for them. I no longer hated them or wanted to hurt them, but I wanted them to know what I had done and how even in that short time my life had been changed so much. I felt they needed to know too because they were just as desperate and messed up inside as I had been. I actually felt sorry for them and wanted to help them! I knew then that God was really real and that He had clearly answered my prayer to make Himself real to me. God had changed the terrible hate in my heart to love! I prayed and asked God to let me share with each of them before I was transferred by the military out-of-town. It was not very easy to get close, one-on-one, with a couple of them because they carried guns most of the time and our relationship had been a little edgy for a while. God did give me the opportunity to share with each one of them personally before I was transferred from Memphis to Oklahoma. The last conversation ended with the person saying to me as he turned to leave, "Well, it looks like you are just high on the Lord now." He knew about the Lord as I had through the years; he even sang in a gospel quartet in his public life.

    I met a lot of people each day as I went on my daily travels through Arkansas, Mississippi and the Memphis area. I started telling everyone what had happened to me, or at least of the changes that God had made in me. I did not tell about what lead up to me turning to God because the sin and circumstances are even still embarrassing after all these years. It is difficult to imagine how I could have lived so long and been completely blind of any presence of God without recognizing it and making some effort to get it worked out with God. As I shared with others, I was not sure just what to share with people since I had attended church from age nine and felt it had not done any good since it had not helped me develop a personal relationship to God with Christ in my heart. During those years of hearing all those sermons three to ten times a week, I never once suspected that I might not be a Christian, but I would readily admit I was not a very good one. As a result, when I started witnessing to people I would just share the new things God was doing in my life and encourage the people to "Just get your Bible out, read it, pray and see what God will do for you." I had become hooked on reading the Bible. That was another big change in my heart after I had prayed that night, the first time I picked up a Bible and started reading it was like a new book. It came alive to me; I could hardly put it down. I carried a small New Testament with the book of Psalms in my back pocket and read it when I stopped to eat, service the car or at any other normally idle time. Government cars in those days did not have radios, so I carried a portable stereo and played gospel music all day. As I continued to read the Scriptures, I began to see phrases like, "changed heart," "new creature," "Christ in us," "if any man have not the Spirit of Christ, he is none of His," and I could understand what these verses meant now that it had happened to me because I had received such dramatic changes in my heart.

CHOOSE FAITH AND GRACE
INTRODUCTION

With as much joy as I was having in my new relationship with God, I started to develop a reverential fear of God as I recognized the possibility of what would have happened to me if I had died during all those years that I thought I was a Christian and was not! I soon started to include in my witness the question as to whether the individual was a Christian, but before they would answer I would explain what I meant by being a Christian. I would ask if they had turned to God with all their heart, asked God to forgive them of their sins, and had invited the Spirit of Christ into their heart and life, and at that time in their life did they know without a doubt that the Spirit of Christ had come into their heart and created in them a new heart. I became alarmed at the responses I would receive: "I'm a Baptist," "I am a Catholic," "I go to church a lot," "I was born in the United States," "My uncle is a preacher," "I just told my wife the other day that we need to start going to church more," and on and on! Very few people understood or had any idea what I was talking about when I would mention the changed heart, especially when I asked them what had changed in their heart and life as a result of them receiving Christ or getting "saved." How could anyone see himself as a sinner, heart filled with sin, invite the Spirit of Christ, love, into his heart and then when He enters into his heart, the person not recognize it? That would be like saying the person was so good in their heart before receiving Christ that Christ coming into their heart did not change anything enough for them to notice the changes. That is ridiculous! Mankind is born filled with sin, and without Christ in their heart, the heart is empty of God or Love. When a person calls out to God with a hurting heart, he should recognize some change if he called with all his heart and received an answer to remove the hurt from his heart. If a person took pain medicine for a hurt arm, leg or foot, he would certainly notice if the pain went away or not. A person can say the words asking forgiveness to get saved from hell but want to hold on to some areas of their life of sin; God does not take or respond to less than a whole heart. It is all or none! *Deuteronomy 4:29 and Jeremiah 29:13 both state, "And ye shall seek me, and find me, when ye shall search for me with all your heart."*

CHOOSE FAITH AND GRACE
INTRODUCTION

If anyone recognizes doubt of their salvation or doubt of whether they have received the changed heart while reading this book, make it a top priority to seek, read the Bible, and pray(talk to God) until God confirms to you somehow that Christ lives in your heart. It is too serious to have any doubt of your relationship with God. Jesus says in *Matthew 7:21-23, "Not everyone that saith unto me, Lord, Lord, shall enter into the kingdom of heaven; but he that doeth the will of my Father which is in heaven. (22) Many will say to me in that day, Lord, Lord, have we not prophesied in thy name? and in thy name have cast out devils? And in thy name done many wonderful works? (23) And then will I profess unto them, I never knew you: depart from me, ye that work iniquity."* If the main thing that comes to your mind when you think of being a Christian is how long you have worked in the church teaching a class, being a deacon, how long you have preached, led the music or some other activity, you should seek the Lord until you get the total assurance that Christ lives in your heart. When God reveals to you that Christ lives in your heart, you will know it, and you will want everyone else to know it. You will not have to make yourself share it with others; you will have to keep yourself from sharing if you do not speak out. Do not just start confessing that Christ lives in your heart because the Bible says so without the assurance from God that He lives in you personally. Talk to Him! He will let you know because He wants a personal fellowship with you; in fact, that is why He created us all. God instructs His people in *Isaiah 34:16, "Seek ye out of the book of the Lord, and read: no one of these shall fail..."* My prayer for everyone who reads this book is that you will gain the full assurance of Christ in your heart for salvation and that you are a child of God before you finishing reading it.

As I studied to become a better witness and to be better able to answer peoples' questions, I started reading books of different writers and listening to radio and TV programs of many different denominational beliefs. I found there was a great confusion in the Christian community about almost all of the basic beliefs: salvation, faith, gifts of the Spirit, baptisms, and even which copies of

CHOOSE FAITH AND GRACE
INTRODUCTION

the Bible are inspired and which might be of the "devil." How on earth are people of our society who have not been blessed by being raised in a Godly home by Godly parents or guardians going to be able to evaluate from what they hear broadcast on mainline radio and TV, what they need to do, or where they should go to develop a relationship with God if they ever decide they might want to "find" or seek God. I have met young people in their 20's and 30's who not only have not read a Bible but do not even have a Bible. The scary part of this is that there are millions of people in our society that are desperately hurting inside that do not see a personal need for Christianity in their lives or a need to read the Bible because the Christian image is so weak and confusing. The confusion presented by radio and television preachers is a reflection of what is being taught by the various denominational schools and seminaries across our country. People are attending the seminaries not to study to learn the true, Pure Word of God, Christ, but to learn how to interpret and proclaim the Word according to the beliefs of their particular seminary or group in clever or more interesting ways. Christians should be looked to for wisdom when problems arise; yet in our society, people have started blaming "right-wing Christians" (those who believe the Bible) as being the cause of society's problems.

If the special Ambassadors for Christ that are called to be preachers, evangelists and teachers would determine to be more careful and specific in their messages to use the true, Pure Word of God, many more "lost" or "unchurched" people in our society would want to turn to God because He would be working more in their hearts through the messages. The God of the Bible is not being represented very well by our Christian society. Everyone has a void or emptiness in his heart and a desire to fill the emptiness which is created by God, and only the Love of God, Christ, can fill the emptiness to make us a complete being. The Bible states in Ephesians 4:4,13 that these leaders are charged with helping the body of Christ grow into the unity of the one faith. There are not many faiths; there is only one faith. Ministers of all Christian denominations and groups should be studying how to obtain and join together

CHOOSE FAITH AND GRACE
INTRODUCTION

in the one true faith which leads to the grace of God that creates our new changed heart at salvation. Instead, churches are splitting even more today over beliefs about gays, women ministers, prosperity, gifts of the Spirit and baptisms, yet I have not seen any different denominations unite because of coming in agreement or unity of faith on any particular subject or belief. Many ministers who study and try to teach about faith are even criticized by some ministers as radicals so that others possibly shy away from the subject of faith and rarely mention it.

Our Christian community needs a revival of the basics of Christianity. The gospel is clearly stated in *1 Corinthians 15:1-4, "Moreover, brethren, I declare unto you the gospel which I preached unto you, which also ye have received, and wherein ye stand; (2) By which also ye are saved, if ye keep in memory what I preached unto you, unless ye have believed in vain. (3) For I delivered unto you first of all that which I also received, how that Christ died for our sins according to the Scriptures; (4) And that He was buried, and that He rose again the third day according to the Scriptures."* Even though there is probably not total agreement, most of us might agree that a person does not have to know much to become a Christian; that a desperate person laying in the gutter of skid-row could call with all their heart to God and God in His Mercy would respond. The Apostle Paul states in *2 Corinthians 3:16, "Nevertheless when it (the heart) shall turn to the Lord, the vail shall be taken away."* After we receive salvation, we are all Ambassadors for Christ, 2 Corinthians 5:20, and whether we are preachers, teachers or just ordinary Christians, we should be studying God's Word to be an Ambassador capable of sharing God's Pure Word to all people in our daily lives. Every Christian should be seeking God personally to be a better witness in sharing clearly the one faith, grace, mercy, trust, hope, sin, salvation, and other Christian concepts which build upon our perfect, basic foundation of Christ in us. The better we each can understand the basic fundamental beliefs, the better the spiritual house we will be able to built on the perfect foundation, *1 Peter 2:5 says, "Ye also, as lively stones, are built up a spiritual house, an holy priesthood, to offer up spiritual sacrifices, acceptable to God by Jesus Christ."* The Apostle Paul says that we should be very concerned how we build on our foundation of Christ because we are all going to have to answer to God for our works performed while here on earth. Paul states in *1 Corinthians 3:9 – 15, "For we are labourers together with God: yeare God's husbandry, ye are God's building. (10) According to the grace of God which is given unto me, as a wise masterbuilder, I have laid the foundation, and another buildeth thereon. But let every man take heed how he buildeth thereupon. (11) For other foundation can no man lay than that is laid, which is Jesus Christ. (12) Now if any man build upon this foundation gold, silver, precious stones, wood, hay, stubble; (13) Every man's work shall be made manifest: for the day shall declare it, because it shall be revealed by fire; and the fire shall try every man's work of what sort it is. (14) If any man's work abide which he hath built thereupon, he shall receive a reward. (15) If any man's work shall be burned, he shall suffer loss: but he himself shall be saved; yet so as by fire."* We each will have to answer at the Judgment Seat of Christ for how we have used our gifts and talents. The Apostle Paul states in *2 Corinthians 5:10-11, "For we must all appear before the judgment seat of Christ; that every one may receive the things done in his body, according to that he hath done, whether it be good or bad."* God has promised to forget our sins when we ask and He forgives them. Therefore, the only bad that can be at the judgment seat of Christ are our unforgiven sins which will include failing to seek God's special calling for our lives and not using our gifts and talents to reach out to others.

We each are responsible for speaking God's Pure Word as a personal Ambassador of God, regardless of our denominational affiliation. If we change His Word in any way or deny any of His Word that we know to be true, He will not back what we say, and we will be out of fellowship with Him because He and His Word are the same, as stated in *Proverbs 30:5-6, "Every Word of God is pure: He is a shield unto them that put their trust in Him. (6) Add thou not*

CHOOSE FAITH AND GRACE
INTRODUCTION

unto His Words, lest He reprove thee, and thou be found a liar." God's Word is Christ, the third part of the Trinity, which is most often called the Holy Spirit. God is so concerned about His Pure Word that in *Psalms 138:2 the Scripture says, "I will worship toward thy holy temple, and praise thy name for thy lovingkindness and for thy truth: for thou hast magnified thy Word above all thy name."* There must be a serious effort made throughout Christianity to bring differing Christian beliefs into the unity of one faith which comes from hearing and accepting God's Pure Word. God will not tell denominations different Words. Presently, our Christian community is broken, confused and unconcerned about coming together in unity; all of the different groups are doing their own thing, and none are concerned about trying to bring the body of Christ together in unity of the one faith based on His Pure Word. Therefore, for God to pour out His Spirit and change our nation, the Christian community must come together and seek the unity of the Pure Word, not just what has been passed down with so much confusion by our forefathers.

My question for us at this point is this: "Do we have the love in our heart for God that we will be willing to follow Him through His Pure Word, Christ, regardless of what others in our family or denomination chose to do? We each must examine the commitment we made at salvation that we would surrender our lives to Christ, God's living Word. We as groups of people cannot change back what has been set in motion in our country recently because too many changes have already been initiated that would be impossible for us to change back, but God could make a lot of changes if we loved Him and His Word enough to seek and accept His Pure Word! In 2 Kings 20:1-11, God backed up His prophet Isaiah by moving the earth and sun so that the shadow moved backwards ten degrees on the sun dial when King Hezekiah asked for a sign that God had spoken through Isaiah. God would back up the Christians in our country too if we were united in speaking His Pure Word. God stated in *Isaiah 44:24 - 26, "Thus saith the Lord...(26) That confirmeth the Word of His servant, and performeth the counsel of His messengers..."* If we Christians will join together and seek and share God's Pure Word, God will back up His Word that we speak and the Christian counsel we give to our society! The choice is ours: Continue in the Christian confusion and allow our country to fall, or be willing to turn to the Lord for His Pure Word regardless of our denominational beliefs. If anyone is not willing to make the necessary effort and changes, then there is no reason to read any further in this book.

Christian Leaders Are Ignorant Of Biblical Faith and Grace!

Thousands of Christian Doctors of Theology and lesser educated preachers in our country who are supposedly experts in Hebrew, Greek, Latin and the English language do not even know the simple Biblical definitions of faith and grace. How can I say this when I do not know all of them? The TV and radio preachers, teachers, and guests on live discussion and praise shows reflect what is being taught in the seminaries and other Bible schools across our country. What makes this so important and scary is that they cannot possibly understand correctly any Scripture which contains the words faith or grace if they do not know the correct meanings. One of the most important Scriptures of salvation is *Ephesians 2:8, "For by grace are ye saved through faith,..."* and every Christian should grow to understand and be able to explain it clearly. **Although people can get "saved" without knowing the definitions of faith or grace by seeking God and calling out to Christ with all their hearts, it would be much simpler and more people would want to become Christians if our leaders, especially all of those who for years have been living off charitable contributions, were able to explain the Scriptures of faith and grace clearly and correctly.** As mentioned earlier, we are all Ambassadors for Christ, but preachers, pastors and evangelists who have made a full-time ministry of their service for the Lord should certainly know the basics beliefs of Christianity and be able to teach them clearly, for they will be held to a greater

CHOOSE FAITH AND GRACE
INTRODUCTION

accountability as stated in *James 1:1, "My brethren, be not many masters(teachers), knowing that we shall receive the greater condemnation."* Ministers are also charged by Scriptures to bring us, the Christian body or church, into the unity of the one faith as stated in *Ephesians 4:11 - 13, "And He gave some, apostles; and some, prophets; and some, evangelists; and some, pastors and teachers; (12) For the perfecting of the saints, for the work of the ministry, for the edifying of the body of Christ: (13) Till we all come in the unity of the faith, and of the knowledge of the Son of God, unto a perfect man, unto the measure of the stature of the fullness of Christ."*

I have heard Dr. Dobson, Dr. Duplantis, Dr. Hagee, Dr. McArthur, Dr. Kennedy, Dr. Price, Dr. Schuller, Dr. Stanley, Kenneth Copeland, Benny Hinn, Pat Robertson, Andrew Wommack, T.D. Jakes and Hank Hanegraaff (who as the Bible-Answer-Man is supposed to know-it-all) along with many others on national TV and radio programs misuse the words faith and grace so badly that they create more confusion and cause more harm than if they had not said anything at all. Their lack of knowledge and understanding of basic definitions of faith and grace also causes them to unknowingly be confused about other biblical truths which are based on faith and grace. The lack of understanding and the resulting confusion in our Christian society is being evidenced by the demise of the Christian influence in our nation and by the fact that even the few ministers mentioned above are not in unity and agreement of the one faith either. With all of these preachers' great confessions of faith and grace, there is very little noticeable response in our society of God backing up and honoring what they are saying and claiming. Again, *Proverbs 30:5-6 states, "Every Word of God is pure: He is a shield unto them that put their trust in Him. (6) Add thou not unto His words, lest He reprove thee, and thou be found a liar."* This Scripture explains what is presently happening in our society: Christianity has added and taken so much from God's Word that it is full of lies and liars. God is not backing up and confirming the words of our Christian leaders because they are unintentionally, probably through ignorance in most cases, adding so much

CHOOSE FAITH AND GRACE
INTRODUCTION

impurity to God's Word by their lack of knowledge and understanding of faith and grace. God told His people in *Amos 8:11, "Behold, the days come, saith the Lord God, that I will send a famine in the land, not a famine of bread, nor a thirst for water, but of hearing the Words of the Lord."* We have a famine of God's "Pure Word" in our land, and God has not caused or sent it. Many of the denominations and other groups have accepted beliefs formulated several hundred years ago without caring enough to seek the Lord for confirmation of whether it is His "Pure Word" or not.

In the following material, I will show first that the definitions used by most ministers for faith and grace in worldwide television and radio broadcasts are completely incorrect. I have a list of the statements, dates and broadcasts when the ministers I have referred to have made the false statements about faith and grace. Many of these men are influencing millions of people all around the world. I know none of us is perfect, but ministers should be so concerned as special Ambassadors for Christ that they make sure they respect and are speaking God's Pure Word and not preaching messages which contain error just to support denominational beliefs, religious clichés or jokes. We are warned that masters (teachers) will be held by God to a higher standard in James Chapter 1, verse 1, stated before. God's Will is for ministers of all denominations to be trying to bring all Christians into the ONE faith mentioned above in Ephesians Chapter 4. It is not God's Will for us to have all of these divided groups with so many opposing beliefs. The devil has caused all of this confusion in Christianity through the pride of our past and present Christian leaders. Since in Ephesians 2:8 above it states we are "saved by grace through faith," I will discuss faith first.

CHOOSE FAITH...

One of the most common beliefs throughout all the many Christian denominations is that God has blessed mankind with a definition of faith in *Hebrews 11:1, which states, "Now faith is the substance of things hoped for, the evidence of things not seen."* This would be awesome, except that Hebrews 11:1 is not a definition! It only talks about faith but does not define faith, a very critical difference. Hebrews 11:1 only says that when our hopes are fulfilled, we have evidence that unseen faith was the substance present and manifested to fulfill the hopes. It tells us how to recognize the manifestation of faith in our lives. Faith is the unseen substance fulfilling our hopes even though we cannot see it. This is true, but it is not a definition of faith.

For example, suppose we look out the window of our house and see in the field that our windmill blades are turning. We could say, "Wind is the substance fulfilling our hope, to turn the blades, which is the evidence of things unseen, the wind." Wind causes the blades to turn, thus, fulfilling our hope. Because our hope is being fulfilled, that is evidence the unseen wind is manifested at the windmill performing the actions necessary to turn the blades. We can then say, "Wind is the substance of things hoped for, the evidence of things not seen." This does not define wind; it only tells when unseen wind is manifested at the windmill. To define wind, we would have to talk about movement of air molecules.

Similarly, when we flip a light switch and the light brightens we could say, "Electricity is the substance that fulfilled our hope for the light to come on. We have evidence the unseen electricity is present because we see the shining light." Therefore, "Electricity is the substance of things hoped for, the evidence of things not seen." This statement does not define electricity. It only talks about electricity and tells that electricity is manifested or present in the light if our hope is fulfilled by the light shining. We would have to discuss charged ions and electron movement to define electricity.

Imagine the condition of meteorology and electrical engineering if universities taught the above "definitions" of wind as "the substance of things hoped for, to turn windmill blades, even though we cannot see the wind," and electricity was defined as "the substance of things hoped for, to turn on lights, even though we cannot see the electricity." Weather forecasts would then really be more of a joke than they sometimes are today, and we would still be using kerosene lamps instead of electrical lights. As foolish as the above "definitions" of wind and electricity are, most of our Christian community is using a similar ridiculous definition of faith, Hebrews 11:1. Our leaders talk about faith but do not know what faith is! There is no way our Christian leaders can lead us, the body of Christ, together into unity of one faith when so many do not even know what faith is themselves. A few might be close to correct but, with the thousands of others giving out so many different made up definitions or beliefs, how is a concerned lost person supposed to know who to believe.

Preachers give almost any imaginable discussion on Christian TV and radio trying to explain Hebrews 11:1 as "God's definition of faith." This erroneous "definition" with the many personal interpretations is a reflection of the errors being taught in the seminaries, Bible schools and what is being preached across our nation. God will not back up these teachings about faith by our Christian community because He only backs up and honors His Pure Word. Any teaching based on Hebrews 11:1 being the definition of faith will have a foundation of error which will not lead to the truth of faith or God's Pure Word.

Two of the main themes throughout the Bible are God's love toward mankind and our response to His love. God has sent prophets, priests, His Son Jesus, the disciples and many other people with special callings of service to reach out in love to mankind; but most people have rejected God, His Word and His love. Our response to God's love must be in or through faith to be pleasing and acceptable to God. Therefore, our understanding of the faith Scriptures, God's Word, has a great influence on how each of us chooses to respond to God. I believe if faith were taught in a clear understandable manner that more people would turn to God and invite His Spirit into their heart.

CHOOSE FAITH AND GRACE
CHOOSE FAITH

Another theme throughout the Bible is that the devil will do everything he can to block our positive response to God or try to confuse us so we respond incorrectly. The devil tried for centuries to keep the Scriptures from common people. Now that we have the Scriptures, he does as much as he can to confuse the meaning of the words, so we will not understand them properly. The common, everyday meaning of many biblical words such as: faith, hope, unbelief, mercy, grace and charity, has changed through the years because they are being used by society in unscriptural contexts. I have already shown that even though Hebrews 11:1 is a true statement, it is not a definition of faith. It only talks about faith! There is a great difference in talking about something and explaining its meaning or definition. We need to find from the Scriptures the true Biblical definitions or meanings of the above words and be sure not to use the words as they have been changed by society.

The better we understand faith, the better we will be able to respond positively to God and do those things that are pleasing in His sight. While reading the following material you will learn many concepts of faith, and I will explain what faith is, from where it comes, and what we need to do to grow in faith. We will be able to grow in faith anytime we desire and have the confidence that we are walking by faith and are pleasing to God. The confusion about what faith is and what we must do to grow in faith will be cleared up. This new understanding will bring great peace and eliminate many concerns you may have about your future.

Faith is a necessary ingredient in each Christian's life. Everything we receive from God comes to us through faith, except when God intervenes through His great mercy and bypasses the normal channel. We are instructed in Romans 1:17 that "the just shall live by faith." In Hebrews 11:6 we are told that it is impossible to please God without faith, and in Romans 14:23 we find that everything not of faith is sin. Ephesians 2:8 states that we are saved or receive salvation by grace through faith, and Hebrews 6:12 states that we, the heirs of promise, inherit God's great and precious promises by faith. In Ephesians 6:16 we have a Shield of Faith to quench all the fiery darts of the wicked one, and in 1 John 5:4 we obtain victory over the world by our faith. Therefore, it is easy to see that our Christian walk must be a daily walk of faith if we desire to please God. Faith is also one of the basic subjects that all ministers of the Gospel and most Christians should be able to explain clearly to anyone they meet.

As I studied about faith, I wanted to know how I could grow in faith, and specifically what I could do right now, without waiting for a feeling or to get in the mood, that would help increase my faith. Something surprising happened as I studied about faith. God caused me to look more closely at the meanings of doubt and unbelief. Until this time, when I would come across either of the words doubt or unbelief in the Scripture text, I would simply recognize that they were bad and I should avoid them if possible. Consequently, I would continue reading without giving the words much additional thought. After the Lord showed me that there was such a great difference between doubt and unbelief, I was led into a clearer understanding of faith and the relationships between the words doubt, unbelief and faith.

I will first take you through an investigation of doubt by studying the basic identifying characteristics and then explaining how to eliminate doubt. In dealing with doubt, we will discuss seeking God to find His Will or Word for the situation and then investigate the importance of our two possible responses to God's answer or His Pure Living Word. When God's Will is revealed to us, we will never again be the same, for we must make a binary choice to accept or to reject; there is no in-between response.

If we choose to reject God's Will or Word, as the children of Israel did when they refused to cross over the Jordan River into the Promised Land, we will be choosing to be in a condition of unbelief, which is willful disobedience. The Scripture in *Hebrews 3:19 states, "So we see that they could not enter in because of unbelief."* The children of Israel failed to enter into the Promised Land because of unbelief, not doubt. They all knew it was God's Will for them to enter the Promised Land, so they were not in doubt. Doubt is when you do not know God's Will. Unbelief is when you know God's Will but choose of your own free will to reject His Will or Word. Doubt is a head problem. Unbelief is a heart problem of knowing God's Will, but not caring, trusting or loving Him enough to accept and obey His Will, the Living Word, Christ.

Choose Faith and Grace
Choose Faith

Unbelief that comes from the willful rejection of God's Will or Living Word, Christ, is from an evil heart as stated in *Hebrews 3: 12,"Take heed, brethren, lest there be in any of you an evil heart of unbelief, in departing from the living God."* The Scripture is referring to the children of Israel not trusting God enough to obey and cross the Jordon even though they all knew it was God's Will. It is also possible to be in ignorant unbelief without an evil heart against God because of believing false teachings like the Apostle Paul before he met Jesus on the road to Damascus, *1 Timothy 1:13 says, "Who(Paul) was before a blasphemer, and a persecutor, and injurious: but I obtained mercy, because I did it ignorantly in unbelief."* Our Christian community is burdened down with both types of unbelief. Many Christians have refused God's personal call for them to teach classes, work with children, visit prisons, and on-and-on. Other Christians have lived in false teachings which result in unbelief for so long that they have become comfortable in their rituals. For those who desire a closer walk with God, the choice of accepting God's Will or Word to faith is the only pleasing response. If we reject any of God's revealed Will or Word to us, we will be in unbelief and out of fellowship with God until we humble ourselves, ask forgiveness and accept His Word, Christ, whom we earlier rejected.

Faith is the result of accepting God's Living Word in our hearts, which we already believe in our heads intellectually. Unbelief with the evil heart is the rejection of God's Word, or the refusal to accept God's Living Word into our hearts while believing and knowing it to be true intellectually. A head knowledge or intellectual belief comes when we recognize something as true, a fact, God's Will or Word. Our response is either to faith or to unbelief, depending on whether we choose to accept or to reject the intellectual belief into our hearts.

The power of God comes with choosing positively according to, and in agreement with, God's Will, or by choosing to accept God's Living Word, Christ, into our heart to faith. Faith for a particular situation does not exist until we make our choice to accept and receive the Living Word into our heart. When we choose to accept, God puts His Spirit of Christ, the Living Words which He has just spoken to us, in our hearts and Christ is then our strength and the Spirit of Faith or measure of faith for the particular situation. It is easy to see now why we cannot please God without faith because we are rejecting Christ, the Living Word, when we reject any of His Word to us, whether it is to teach a class, to preach, to help a neighbor or to do whatever He speaks or asks because His Words to us is Christ.

The relationships of doubt, seeking, belief, unbelief, faith, hope and trust will be discussed with related Scriptures as we investigate each of these areas, beginning with doubt.

DOUBT

Doubt is being in a state or condition of being faced with a problem in which we are unsure what we are to do or when we have two or more possible choices from which we must select only one. For example, we feel called to teach in Sunday school, but we are uncertain which of the two classes needing a teacher would be God's Will for us. We may lack confidence so much in our ability to teach a class that the fear of failure will cause us to refuse both classes. Lack of confidence, after God has called us, is evidence of doubting that God can or will provide for us as we walk His path. Doubt opens the door. Then the devil comes in with the tormenting spirit of fear or worry to scare us away from God's Will.

Fear is the devil trying to torment and keep us so busy fighting the fear that we miss God's Will or Word for our particular situation or problem. The Scriptures state in *2 Timothy 1:7, "For God hath not given us the spirit of fear; but of power, and of love, and of a sound mind."* The spirit of fear is not a spirit from the devil; it is the devil himself. As Christians we are Spirit, soul (mind and emotions) and physical body. Fear is the spirit of the devil; fear is not an emotion, although fear causes us to have extreme emotions of terror, worry and confusion. We fight the devil by seeking God in the area that we doubt about God. In *1 Peter 5:8 the Scripture states, "Be sober, be vigilant; because your adversary the devil, as a roaring lion, walketh about seeking whom he may devour."* If the devil can scare us enough to keep us from finding God's Will or from doing God's Will when we know it, then he will have the advantage in the situation as stated in 2 Corinthians 2:10-11 that we must forgive others lest we give satan the advantage. Any time we neglect God's Word through our choice or ignorance we give satan the advantage in the situation. Regardless how scary circumstances may appear in the natural, if we want God's power and deliverance, we must accept and obey God's Word to faith, which will mean that we must trust God's Word to us and stand against the devil (fear). If God asks us to teach a class or lead a devotional, we must face the fear and trust God to help and provide our needs as we carry out whatever He has asked of us. The Scripture states in *James 4:7, "Submit yourselves therefore to God. Resist the devil, and he will flee from you."* We must always remember that fear is the devil, but when we recognize fear he is only a symptom of our problem. Every time we experience or recognize fear let it be a red flag to remind us that we should ask ourselves, "What about God do I doubt?" We will find that the doubt "door" which we have opened and let the devil in is our doubt that God will protect, provide for, guide, heal, deliver, or even save us. We will be able to identify something about God or His promises that we doubt which is allowing the devil to come in and torment us. The solution is not to go to a deliverance ministry to be set free of fear. The solution is to respond to fear like Jehoshaphat did when he was told that he was surrounded by three armies in *2 Chronicles 20:3, "And Jehoshaphat feared, and set himself to seek the Lord, and proclaimed a fast throughout all Judah."* Only our awareness of God's presence and our obedience to His Word will give us the confidence to stand strong when the devil tries to scare us away from doing God's Will. Fear is the symptom; doubting God is the problem! We should each remember from now own when we recognize fear, worry or excessive concern, to make it a habit to ask ourselves, "What is it about God that I am doubting?" Then, we need to set ourselves to seek the Lord as Jehoshaphat did to be delivered from the three armies. Do not wait until surrounded by great concerns or huge mountains. The Apostle Paul instructs us in *Philippians 4:6, "Be careful for nothing; but in everything by prayer and supplication with thanksgiving let your requests be made known unto God."* Continuing to seek God immediately when concerns arise will lead to a walk of victory as stated in *1 John 5:4, "For whatsoever is born of God overcometh the world: and this is the victory that overcometh the world (satan, devil, fear), even our faith."*

Lack of conviction is another evidence of doubt. Lack of conviction in an area is the result of not knowing God's Will. We may be right in our belief, but if we are not sure that it is God's Will, our conviction will not be solid or firm

CHOOSE FAITH AND GRACE
CHOOSE FAITH - DOUBT

in times of trials. This situation could occur when our beliefs have been taught to us by trusted family and close friends, and we have never taken the time to seek God for His confirmation. In this case, we would be living on second hand knowledge and would not have the personal conviction to stand against most trials the devil would bring. Living on second hand knowledge may be why the devil tempted Eve instead of Adam in the Garden of Eden. In Genesis 2:15-17, God told Adam not to eat of the tree of the knowledge of good and evil. Later in Genesis 2, God formed Eve. The Scripture never states that Eve asked for confirmation about not eating of the tree or that she had received a personal Word from God, so she might have been living on second hand knowledge. We must seek the Lord about our beliefs until they become personal firsthand knowledge between us and God.

Many people lack a personal conviction of what God's Will is concerning present-day issues, such as tithing, smoking, drinking, abortion or women wearing makeup, short dresses and many other areas. We will continue to be in doubt about these topics until we personally seek God and He reveals His Will to us in that particular area. It seems to me that most people I have known instead of seeking God just try to pick the most common beliefs that will create the least disturbance among the friends and relatives they are associated with the most.

Doubt is very harmful, even deadly, to Christians. The Scripture in *James 1:6–7* points out how doubt in our hearts, even though we may be saying great words of faith, will cause our prayers to be unanswered, "*But let him ask in faith, not wavering. For he that wavereth is like a wave of the sea driven with the wind and tossed. For let not that man think that he shall receive anything of the Lord.*" Praying in doubt is not pleasing to God, unless you are praying to get out of the doubt. Maybe the following example will clarify what James is talking about when he said to not pray in doubt.

A man who was partially paralyzed down one side of his face stated to me, "I'm claiming my healing by faith." As we talked for a few minutes, he made the comment that his partial paralysis might just be his "thorn in the flesh." I told him he could not claim his healing by faith because he was in doubt. He was not sure of God's Will, whether it was God's Will to heal him or

CHOOSE FAITH AND GRACE
CHOOSE FAITH - DOUBT

if it was his "thorn in the flesh." Faith cannot exist when more than one possibility exists because for faith to exist, we have to be able to say God has told us which is His Will. Doubt and faith cannot exist together. Either God has spoken or doubt remains. I told the man he must first pray and find which possibility was in fact God's Will, and then pray in faith accordingly. He was saying the expected words of faith: that he was claiming his healing. In his heart, he believed that the condition could be his "thorn in the flesh," so that God would not heal him. He did not recognize that he was living in doubt until our discussion. Many people are saying great "words of faith" but have doubt in their hearts.

Another person says he believes it is God's Will to heal everyone, but he believes it may not be God's Will to heal this person now. So he confesses faith that God can heal everyone, but in fact, doubts, or is not sure, that God will heal in any specific situation. Therefore, in praying for a specific person's sickness, he would be unsure and doubt whether it is God's Will to heal in that particular situation. He could not pray a prayer of faith for this particular individual since he is unsure of what God's Will is in this specific situation.

Many pray, "Lord, if it be Thy will, please heal brother or sister so-and-so." The "if" clearly states that the person is in doubt and does not know God's Will. When Jesus prayed in the garden "Thy will be done," He was not in doubt about God's Will. He was submitting Himself to God's Will. He knew it was His Father's Will for Him to go to the cross. He was not questioning whether it was God's Will or not. In **Mark 14:36 and Luke 22:42, Jesus prayed, "Father, if thou be willing, remove this cup from me: nevertheless, not my will, but thine, be done."** Jesus knew His Father's Will. There was no element of doubt in His prayer, as when people pray, "If it be Thy will." Doubt and faith cannot exist together. In **Matthew 21:21, Jesus says, "Verily I say unto you, If ye have faith, and doubt not, ye shall not only do this which is done to the fig tree, but also if ye shall say unto this mountain, Be thou removed, and be thou cast into the sea and it shall be done."** Many miracles of healing, financial blessings, and even salvation for lost loved ones are blocked in the lives of sincere Christians due to hidden or covered-over doubt. Doubt is a killer! Seek God until He gets you out of doubt.

CHOOSE FAITH AND GRACE
CHOOSE FAITH - DOUBT

Doubt is sin according to Romans 14:23 which states that everything not of faith is sin. Therefore, we must not be slack but diligent in searching the Scriptures about areas of our life to see if we are standing firmly on the Scriptures, or on what our particular group says. We all are going to have doubt when faced with unfamiliar situations of life. It is not sin to have the doubt; it only becomes sin if we continue to live with the doubt and do not take it to God in prayer. Since God knows that so many people turn to alcohol, drugs, sex, money, power or cults when faced with problems, He has promised to do good to those who will seek Him. The Scripture states in *Lamentations 3:25, "The Lord is good unto them that wait for Him, to the soul that seeketh Him."*

Confusion is another evidence or sign of doubt and the devil. *James 3:16 states, "For where envying and strife is, there is confusion and every evil work."* Envying, strife and confusion are signs the devil is present. In *Acts 2:11–13 the Scriptures state, ". . . we do hear them speak in our tongues the wonderful works of God. (12) And they were all amazed, and were in doubt, saying one to another what meaneth this? (13) Others mocking said, These men are full of new wine."* The people knew they were all hearing in their own language, but were confused and in doubt as to what was taking place. Peter was in doubt when God spoke to him three times by the visions in *Acts 10:16–18, "This was done thrice . . . now while Peter doubted in himself what this vision which he had seen should mean. . . ."* Peter was uncertain as to what God's message in the visions meant. Jesus speaks again of doubt in *Luke 12:28, ". . . how much more will he clothe ye, O ye of little faith? And seek not ye what ye shall eat, or what ye shall drink, neither be ye of doubtful mind."*

Being doubtful will cause us to miss God's provisions. We inherit the promises of God through faith, acceptance and obedience to His Word. Many Christians are missing blessings that belong to the children of God as joint heirs with Jesus because they doubt the promises are for today, or they may have been taught God does not work in personal lives as He did in "Bible days." If you have been taught that God does not work in the lives of people today like He did in the lives of people in the Bible, then start seeking and ask God to show you how personal He wants to be with you. He will answer and clear up or remove any doubt because He wants a close personal relationship with all people. No one can prove it to you though because it would only be our words. For anyone to learn the truth, they must seek God and let Him make His presence personal to them. God will reveal Himself to those who are concerned enough to seek with all their heart and ask Him because Jesus says in **Matthew 7:7-8, "Ask, and it shall be given you; seek, and ye shall find; knock, and it shall be opened unto you: (8) for every one that asketh receiveth; and he that seeketh findeth; and to him that knocketh it shall be opened."**

Characteristics or symptoms, which help us recognize doubt in our life, include but are not limited to lack of conviction, uncertainty, indecision, fear, worry, apprehension, and confusion. Doubt opens the door for the devil's, fear, torment and worry. When doubt is resolved by hearing from God, the other conditions are settled or removed. Doubt in itself is not a sin, but the way we respond to doubt determines whether it becomes sin to us or not. Situations will come up daily where we will not know God's Will, but He expects us to turn to Him in prayer. Moses often fell before the Lord for help. Gideon kept asking God in Judges, Chapters 6 and 7, until God removed all of his doubt and fear. When Jeshoshaphat feared in 2 Chronicles 20:3, he turned to the Lord for help. In Daniel 5:12 and 16, Daniel is referred to as a dissolver of doubts, but he states in *Daniel 2:28 that, "There is a God in heaven that revealeth secrets. . . ."* Daniel gave God all the credit for his ability to interpret the king's dreams and resolve doubts.

If we recognize doubt and do not take it to the Lord to find His Will, then it will be counted to us as sin. *James 4:17 states, "Therefore to him that knoweth to do good, and doeth it not, to him it is sin."* The Scriptures never say that God will bless just a little bit or an ounce of doubt because where doubt of any amount exists there is no faith for that particular area. To be able to claim something by faith, we must be able to say without any doubt, "God told me this," therefore, not even a small bit of doubt could still be present. God will not bless or respond positively to prayer when there is unrecognized or unadmitted doubt. When a person does not know God's Will, he may say great "words of faith," hoping God will respond to what he honestly believes to be God's Will, and then be disappointed or confused when God does not react according to his incorrect beliefs. Being seriously wrong will not be imputed as righteousness or faith. God states in *Hosea 4:6, "My people are destroyed for lack of knowledge; because thou has rejected knowledge, I will also reject thee, that thou shalt be no priest to me: seeing thou has forgotten the law of thy God, I will also forget thy children."*

Our generation is the most blessed generation that has lived on the earth. We have modern conveniences that kings of old would envy and fight to obtain. We also have God's Word readily available to read which was unavailable to common people until recently. We will not have any legitimate reason when we have to answer at the Judgment Seat of Christ for staying in doubt when we have so many materials and special helps available to us for use in study and research.

We should set ourselves to seek in every area of our lives to find what God's Will is, then live accordingly. Areas that need to be investigated are salvation, healing, baptism of the Holy Spirit, finances, relationships with family, relationships with lost, manner of dress, entertainment, service, jobs, witnessing, fears, worries, dating, school, careers, and many other activities in which we are spiritually, emotionally, and physically involved in daily. The only correct response to doubt is to seek the Lord, *"For the Lord giveth wisdom: out of His mouth cometh knowledge and understanding," Proverbs 2:6.*

SEEKING

God is pleased when we turn to Him for help or guidance. In 2 Chronicles 19:3, Jehoshaphat was complimented by the prophet of God because he had prepared his heart to seek God. God blesses or is good to those who seek Him, as *Lamentations 3:25 states, "The Lord is good unto them that wait for him, to the soul that seeketh him."* Solomon's son, Rehoboam, was rebuked in *2 Chronicles 12:14, "And he did evil, because he prepared not his heart to seek the Lord."*

Living in doubt and ignorance of God's Word will not relieve anyone of the responsibility to come to know God in a personal relationship while in this physical life. God has promised that if we seek Him with all our heart, He will answer. The Scripture in *Jeremiah 29:13 states, "And ye shall seek me, and find me, when ye shall search for me with all your heart."* The Lord promised Asa in *2 Chronicles 15:2, "The Lord is with you, while ye be with Him; and if ye seek Him, He will be found of you; but if ye forsake Him, He will forsake you."* At the end of his life, Asa forsook God and died of a foot disease while going to all of the doctors in the land; his pride would not let him repent and turn back to God.

Our family and friends will benefit from the blessings God pours out on us for seeking Him. Conversely, our family and friends will miss blessings that they could have received if we fail to seek God's Will. God's Word states in *1 Chronicles 28:8, "Now therefore in the sight of all Israel the congregation of the Lord, and in the audience of our God, keep and seek for all the commandments of the Lord your God: that ye may possess this good land, and leave it for an inheritance for your children after you forever."* To seek means more than to just sit back and be available. Seeking is to search for; to endeavor to obtain; or to make a positive effort to obtain. Seeking will result in an active effort of involvement like looking for lost keys or a lost diamond wedding ring. Depending on the importance we feel about what we are seeking for will determine the time we will invest, and the other things in our life we will set aside as we commit ourselves to seek through to the end. Someday soon for each of us, all that will count will be what we have done through Christ, the Living Word, by our acceptance and obedience of His Word to faith.

Throughout the Old Testament, the children of Israel were instructed to seek God. In *1 Chronicles 16:10–11, the Scriptures say, "Glory ye in his holy name: Let the heart of them rejoice that seek the Lord. Seek the Lord and His strength, seek His face continually."* "Set your heart and your soul to seek the Lord your God" was also the instruction in Asaph's Psalm of Thanksgiving.

God considers it evil and wicked to fail to seek Him because pride is what causes man to desire his own way instead of seeking God's way. Psalm 10:4 states, "The wicked, through the pride of his countenance, will not seek after God. God is not in all his thoughts." God's Word states in *Proverbs 28:5,*

CHOOSE FAITH AND GRACE
CHOOSE FAITH - SEEKING

"Evil men understand not judgment: but they that seek the Lord understand all things." Amos 5:6 states, "Seek the Lord, and ye shall live; lest he break out like fire in the house. . . ." In Hosea 10:12, "For it is time to seek the Lord, till he comes and rains righteousness upon you." The prophet Isaiah states in *Isaiah 55:6, "Seek ye the Lord while He may be found, call ye upon Him while He is near."* Seeking the Lord in areas of our everyday life is something in which each of us should be actively involved.

God has set aside many blessings for only those who will seek Him. *Psalm 34:10 states, "The young lions do lack, and suffer hunger; but they that seek the Lord shall not want any good thing."* Those are called blessed who seek God in *Psalms 119:2, "Blessed are they that keep His testimonies, and that seek Him with the whole heart."* Jesus promised that if we seek, we will find in *Matthew 7:7, "Ask and it shall be given you; Seek, and ye shall find; knock and it shall be opened unto you."* Jesus gave another promise in Matthew 6:33 which is similar to *Psalms 34:10 when He stated, "Seek ye first the kingdom of God, and His righteousness; and all these things shall be added unto you."* If we look at the Scriptures prior to verse 33, we will find that "all these things" means everything that pertains to our life in the Lord. Our spiritual, emotional and physical needs will be supplied if we will seek the Lord and His Will for our lives with our whole hearts.

The Apostle Paul encourages us to seek spiritual gifts so that we may help others in *1 Corinthians 14:12, "Even so ye, forasmuch as ye are zealous of spiritual gifts, seek that ye may excel to the edifying of the church."* Again the Holy Spirit encourages us through the Apostle Paul in *Colossians 3:1–2, "If ye then be risen with Christ, seek those things which are above, where Christ sitteth on the right hand of God. Set your affections on the things above, not on things on the earth."* Here the instruction is that if we call ourselves Christian, we should act like it! Seek to live for the Lord. Find out about Him and His way by seeking spiritual matters. We must take control of our emotions and set them by our choice on things of God. We must control our emotions! We must not allow them to control us!

These Scriptures should be enough to encourage us to get personally involved in seeking God regardless how "unlearned" we may think we are and how unqualified we may feel. Getting to know God, becoming a Christian and walking with God by faith are simple enough that anyone can do them. God made His way simple, so we would all be included. He responds to an honest, seeking heart and will give knowledge, understanding and wisdom to those who come to Him.

The question comes now, "How do I go about seeking God? What can I do this very minute that will draw me closer to God and give me increased understanding of God?" First we should ask God right now to help us open our hearts to His fullness. Ask Him to reveal Himself to us in ways that will not let our emotions or feelings block us from recognizing His presence. We must make a commitment that in our life with the Lord we will receive or accept whatever God speaks to us, regardless of past beliefs or ideas. We must come before the Lord with open hearts and minds to receive whatever He has for us. After we have talked honestly with God and made our commitment to seek and serve Him, *Isaiah 34:16 states, "Seek ye out of the book of the Lord, and read: No one of these shall fail, none shall want her mate; for my mouth it hath commanded, and His Spirit it hath gathered them."*

We could make a list of those areas for which we are concerned and start searching God's Word from cover to cover for what it has to say about each subject. Ask others what they think, but do not take everything they say as the truth. It might help thought if we would at least be open and consider their beliefs as we study the Scriptures. *Daniel stated in Daniel 9:3, "And I set my face unto the Lord God, to seek by prayer and supplications, with fasting, and sackcloth and ashes."*

Fasting is a means of helping us focus on God in prayer and fellowship. If we fast from food, every time we think of food we should pray about our special concern. Again, we may want to fast from cigarettes by giving them up for a fixed period like three days. During our fast every time we desire a cigarette, see someone else smoking, or even have the word cigarette form in our mind, we let that word remind us to pray about our special concern.

Fasting is not just giving up something. Fasting is giving up something that is very special to us so that each time we think of it we will be reminded to pray. We could fast from food, cigarettes, watching television, or many other things that have become a big part of our life. The more we have been involved in or controlled by the area we are fasting from, the more we will be reminded to pray. If we watch television a lot, we would benefit very much by giving up television for three days while substituting prayer and Bible reading during the normal TV watching times.

We could wear a pin or carry an object in our pocket as a reminder when we see it to pray. God gave a similar instruction to the people in *Numbers 15:37–40: "And the Lord spake unto Moses, saying, Speak unto the children of Israel, and bid them that they make them fringes in the borders of their garments throughout their generations, and that they put upon the fringe of the borders a ribbon of blue: And it shall be unto you for a fringe, that ye may look upon it, and remember all the commandments of the Lord, and do them; and that ye seek not after your own heart and your own eyes, after which ye use to go a whoring: that ye may remember, and do all my commandments, and be holy unto your God."* God told the people to wear a ribbon of blue to remind them of Him and His commandments. We should do whatever it takes to allow us to focus on seeking God and separate other things from our life that would hinder our fellowship with God.

Learning to communicate with an "unseen" Spirit is as complicated as an adult who has been blind all his life suddenly being able to see, and then immediately trying to determine the direction the wind is blowing on a blusterous day. Regardless of our background or inexperience in seeking God, He has promised if we seek with an honest desire to know His Will or Word that He will hear and answer. It is the Spirit of God in us that causes us to want His Will, so He certainly will answer and reveal Himself when we seek Him, as stated in *Philippians 2:13: "For it is God which worketh in you both to will and to do His pleasure."*

We seek and wait upon the Lord in each area of our life until we know we have heard from God. We must seek through the Scriptures to find God's promises or instructions for our circumstances. We will get to know God in a personal way like we would other friends. We will find out how He reacts to our prayers, desires, and thoughts. The Scriptures state that our knowledge of

God and Jesus our Lord is very important in our daily walk. *Second Peter 1:2–4 states, "Grace and peace be multiplied unto you through the knowledge of God, and of Jesus our Lord. According as His divine power hath given unto us all things that pertain unto life and godliness, through the knowledge of Him that hath called us to glory and virtue: whereby are given unto us exceeding great and precious promises: that by these we might be partakers of the divine nature, having escaped the corruption that is in the world through lust."*

There are examples in the Scriptures of how we can pray "instructive" type prayers. What I mean by instructive prayers is that we word our questions in a way that when God answers, we know His special will for our circumstance. Two examples of how to word our requests are given in Genesis 24:14 and 1 Samuel 14:9–10.

In Genesis 24:14, the servant asks God to speak through God's choice for a woman to marry Isaac and answer a certain statement, *"Drink, and I will give thy camels drink also."* In 1 Samuel 14:9–10, Jonathan asks God to speak through the Philistines and say, "*Tarry until we come to you,*" or "*Come up unto us"* to tell him whether to stay in his place of hiding or to fight. Notice that when God answered each of the men, they accepted God's answer immediately and responded accordingly. Some other examples of how people worded their requests are given in Numbers 16:30–34; Judges 6:36–40; 2 Kings 20:7–11, and John 11:41–43. These Scriptures are stories of how people prayed and would be a good Bible study during your first fast.

God's promise to us in *Psalm 91:1 is that "He that dwelleth in the secret place of the Most High shall abide under the shadow of the Almighty."* The "secret place of the Most High" is not secret because God hides it from us, but because we must seek to find it. The secret place and the rest of God are only for those who care enough to seek the Lord with all their heart.

In Mark 11:23 when Jesus says for us to "not doubt in our heart," He is saying that we must spend the time on our knees in prayer, fasting, studying the Scriptures and seeking until the Father speaks the Rhema, Living Word, Christ, for our situation or "mountain." When God speaks the Living Word,

Christ, to us, our confession of faith is the Rhema Living Word that God spoke to us to get us out of our doubt. Christ is the Rhema Living Word.

How we know clearly God's Will might be different in many cases, but if we seek with all our hearts, God promises He will tell us. *Hebrews 11:6 states, "But without faith it is impossible to please Him: for he that cometh to God must believe that He is, and that He is a rewarder of them that diligently seek Him."* This Scripture is one that can have two meanings depending on our personal belief. If we do not believe God will answer us, we certainly would not diligently seek Him, and He will not answer. But, if we believe God will answer us and diligently seek Him, He will answer us! This is where the expression of "praying through" originated. Old timers kept seeking and praying and would not give up until they got their answers. "Praying through" is not to find God or get His attention; it is to get our hearts right with Him. The Scriptures state in *Isaiah 59:1-2, "Behold, the Lord's hand is not shortened, that it cannot save; neither His ear heavy, that it cannot hear: (2) But your iniquities have separated between you and your God, and your sins have hid His face from you, that He will not hear."* Naturally, "that He will not hear" means that God will not hear and respond favorably to our request.

If you are one of the people who does not believe God will answer if you diligently seek Him, just give God a chance to prove to you that He will. Write the Scripture down and ask God to show you if He desires to answer you. Ask a few simple requests about things involving your family that you know only God could solve. Continue to pray and seek about those circumstances without setting a time limit to give God an opportunity to reveal Himself to you. God will work wonders when people will open up their hearts to Him and not have a negative or know-it-all attitude toward Him. God says in *Jeremiah 33:3, "Call unto me, and I will answer thee, and shew thee great and mighty things, which thou knowest not."*

When we get to the point in time at which we clearly know God's Will and know we have heard God's Rhema Living Word, this is called the Belief Point.

BELIEF POINT

The Belief Point is when we come to the intellectual belief or knowledge in our head that something is right, true, a fact, God's Will or Word. It can be a very simple truth. For example, suppose God teaches us that we should read His Word and pray daily. When we know God has spoken to us and it is not our imagination, we are at the intellectual point of knowing clearly God's Will in this matter. When God teaches us that we personally should tithe, we are at a Belief Point because we have received the Rhema, Living Word or Christ for our situation.

After we have reached the Belief Point, no doubt exists. This is the "shall not doubt in his heart" condition that Jesus talked about in Mark 11:23. Our confession of faith is to speak out exactly, without adding to or taking from, what God spoke to us to remove our doubt. We now know exactly God's Will and what we should do. God may call us to preach, teach a Sunday school class, visit in hospitals or in prisons. The Apostle Peter says in *2 Peter 1:10 for us to "give diligence to make your calling and election sure; for if ye do these things, ye shall never fail."* We must pray and seek until we can say with confidence, "God told me..." for our situation. We cannot claim faith in a situation, unless we have heard God's Pure Word because as *Romans 10:17 states, "So then faith cometh by hearing, and hearing by the Word of God."*

We must not just hope something is God's Will because it sounds good. Good is not necessarily God. As we serve God, problems will come; that is when we need to know without a doubt in our heart we are doing God's Will as Peter stressed in 2 Peter 1:10. When we know we are doing God's Will, we can turn boldly with confidence to Him for the help and assistance we need, regardless of how big the problem appears. With the confidence that comes with the assurance of our calling, we can claim the promise in *1 John 3:21-22 anytime we have a need, "Beloved, if our heart condemn us not, then have we confidence toward God. (22) And whatsoever we ask, We receive of Him, because we keep His commandments, and do those things that are pleasing in His sight."*

CHOOSE FAITH AND GRACE
CHOOSE FAITH - BELIEF POINT

We must come to an intellectual belief or knowledge of God's Will for the particular situation before we can respond in faith according to God's Will. When we first recognize doubt and start seeking God, we are walking in faith that God will answer, even though we are in doubt about the specific circumstances for which we are seeking. Because we are in doubt about one area does not mean that we are in doubt in other areas. We can be in doubt about which Sunday school class to teach, but as we seek God we have faith in His promise that He will answer us. We trust that He will show us His Will about which class to teach. Still there will come a time when, if we are truly seeking God with all our hearts, we will know His Will. This will be an intellectual knowledge of His Will.

Many people know perfectly well they are sinners and should invite the Spirit of Jesus Christ into their hearts and commit their lives to Him. It is no more than an intellectual knowledge or belief to them because they have refused to do it. *In James 2:19, the intellectual belief is mentioned: "Thou believest that there is one God; thou doest well: the devils also believe, and tremble." In Mark 5:7, the devils confessed Jesus intellectually, ". . . what have I to do with thee, Jesus, thou Son of the most high God? I adjure thee by God, that thou torment me not."* The devils knew perfectly well who Jesus was and His Holy Presence tormented them. Many people today are tormented by the mention of the name of Jesus. All day long they will use His name in curses trying in their pride to lift themselves above Him; but when you mention Jesus' name respectfully, they respond in anger.

Jesus said in *John 14:6, "I am the way, the truth, and the life: no man cometh unto the Father, but by me."* When God teaches us we are sinners and that Jesus is our only answer, just knowing and hearing the intellectual truth does not bring faith for our salvation. We must respond positively to the truth. We must choose to accept the Spirit of Jesus Christ into our hearts, or in other words, we must receive both the truth and love of God's Word into our hearts for salvation. The Scripture states in *2 Thessalonians 2:10, "And with all deceivableness of unrighteousness in them that perish; because they received not the love of the truth, that they might be saved."* The Apostle Paul is saying that they heard and knew the truth, but they rejected the Spirit of Christ or love of the message from their hearts.

CHOOSE FAITH AND GRACE
CHOOSE FAITH - BELIEF POINT

We will never be the same after we reach the point of knowing clearly God's Will or Word. The Bible is filled with hundreds of examples of men who were faced by prophets and priests and confronted with "Thus saith the Lord . . ." Regardless of their wealth, position, talents, or status, they all responded in one of two ways: they either accepted in obedience to faith or rejected in disobedience to unbelief. *Hebrews 4:12 states, "For the Word of God is quick, and powerful, and sharper than any two-edged sword piercing even to the dividing asunder of soul and spirit, and of the joints and marrow, and is a discerner of the thoughts and intents of the heart."* We may act before others one way, but the Lord knows the truth of how we have responded in our heart.

We must accept or reject when we know God's Word. There is no in-between. We may claim great "words of faith," but if we have rejected in our heart, we are in unbelief. For example, we may say, "I know I should be reading my Bible and praying daily, but I just do not have the time." In our heads we know intellectually God's Will. But we are rejecting it from our hearts, or we would find the time to obey and do His Will.

The head knowledge without receipt into the heart shows up in a lot of preachers and church staffs' lives in the way they neglect their families and fail to discipline their children. They know in their heads intellectually what they should be doing, but they reject the beliefs from their hearts as the priest Eli *did when God spoke to him about his sons' behavior. God said in 1 Samuel 3:13, "For I have told him that I will judge his house for ever for the iniquity which he knoweth; because his sons made themselves vile, and he restrained them not."* Many leaders decide that taking time with their children is not really as important as the Scriptures state. God's Word is sharp and cuts deep. We may be putting on a front as though we really love God and are seeking to serve Him, but in our heart when we read His Word, God is not deceived.

God may have called us to preach and no one else knows. We may act as joyful and happy as a "pig in mud," but in our hearts we will never be at rest and at peace with God until we surrender to His Will to preach. Knowing God's Will and then failing to surrender to His Will is unbelief and results in a hardening of our heart to other things of God. Our witnessing will drop off, we

CHOOSE FAITH AND GRACE
CHOOSE FAITH - BELIEF POINT

will cease to enjoy fellowship with God's people, and we will begin to find more enjoyment in things unrelated to God. All of the things of God will remind us about our lack of surrender to His Will.

When we receive from God knowledge of His Will, we must respond. We cannot refuse to respond. The fact that we do not accept His Word to faith automatically means we have rejected to unbelief. Being stubborn or "dragging our feet" to delay accepting God's Word is spoken against by God very harshly in *1 Samuel 15:33 in a message to King Saul, "For rebellion is as the sin of witchcraft, and stubbornness is as iniquity and idolatry. Because thou hast rejected the Word of the Lord, He hath also rejected thee from being king."* Even though we may intend to accept someday, while we delay accepting, we are in the state of unbelief.

The fact that we know we should accept Jesus and want to accept Him at some future time will not save us if we die while rejecting Him now. We either accept or reject; there is no straddling the fence with God. His Word is sharper than a double-edged sword. Jesus said in *Matthew 12:30, "He that is not with me is against me; and he that gathereth not with me scattereth abroad."* If we have not accepted God's special call for our life, we are a scatterer, even though we might be doing a lot of good things and others do not know.

Jesus said in *Mark 9:23, "If thou canst believe, all things are possible to him that believeth."* There are two concerns in this verse that must be addressed. First, Jesus said "all things are possible," not that all things would happen. The difference is that so many people reject God's Word or Will, and many things do not happen that should and could have happened, if they had accepted and obeyed God's Word or Will. Also, we cannot generate a belief by our own power in our head or heart that God will back up unless God has put the belief or Word in us. The Scripture even states that God will not back up what we say if we change God's Word, *Proverbs 30:5-6, "Every Word of God is pure: He is a shield unto them that put their trust in Him. (6) Add thou not unto His Words, lest He reprove thee, and thou be found a liar."*

The next two chapters discuss in depth the two possible responses to God: acceptance of God's Word, Christ, to faith or rejection of Christ to unbelief. Unbelief will be discussed first so there will be continuity with discussing grace following faith.

UNBELIEF

Unbelief is very serious, because it is most often associated with a position of being in opposition of heart or in willful rejection of manifested truth, God's Living Word, Christ. Unbelief is equivalent to looking God in the face and telling Him that we do not care about Jesus' suffering and dying on the cross; we will not teach that class, preach, or do whatever He has asked of us because we prefer our way. Unbelief, skepticism, and disbelief are very closely related, as we will see in the following discussion.

Unbelief, in its purest form, is when God has brought us to a perfect knowledge and understanding of His will; then we, of our own free will, chose to reject in disobedience. The skeptic doubts that one could ever know God's perfect will about anything, and the disbeliever fails through ignorance or confusion to recognize God's will.

Both skepticism and disbelief are subcategories of unbelief because God has promised to reveal His Will to anyone who will seek with all their heart. Even though the skeptic or disbeliever refuses to seek or accept God's Will, he will be held accountable for it. He has allowed himself to be led into unbelief at his own will and is without excuse, as the Apostle Paul states in *2 Timothy 2:25-26, "In meekness instructing those that oppose themselves; if God peradventure will give them repentance to the acknowledging of the truth; (26) and that they may recover themselves out of the snare of the devil, who are taken captive by him (devil) at his (the person's) will."*

We are only taken captive by the devil when we allow it. The devil has no power over us; Jesus has all power and authority, and Jesus has not given any power to the devil. We each have the authority to accept or reject God's Word. God will not make us accept His Word, and the devil cannot keep us from accepting God's Word. All we must do to get out of the captivity of the devil is turn to the Lord with all our heart, ask forgiveness and God will set us free. Our problem is that we must humble ourselves and admit we were wrong when we rejected God's Word when He manifested it to us the first time.

Skepticism is a state of mind or belief that perfect or absolute knowledge is impossible to obtain; therefore, the skeptic will never be able to know with certainty God's Will. The skeptic would say that God only revealed His perfect Will to His special chosen people during "Bible days" and that God no longer works that way in men's lives. To the skeptic, the Bible at the most is little more than a history of how God worked with His people and a collection of good principles we should choose to live by today.

Skeptics would accept a form of godliness but deny the power of God working miracles or giving divine guidance in our daily lives. The skeptic would say that we will always be in a certain amount of doubt, and our walk of faith will be filled or at least sprinkled with doubt. They say that God knows we are weak, and if we just do the best we can, it will be all right in the end.

The result of this philosophy is that we pick out the Scriptures we are comfortable with and then do as we "feel led" or what feels good. Skepticism will cause us to miss God when He speaks to us. The skeptic will be right in that he will always remain in doubt since that is what he believes. The Pharisees were very skeptical of Jesus. They wanted a sign to show them Jesus was who He said He was. However, at the time, they disregarded all of His miracles as evidence.

God will remove honest doubt from open-hearted people, *". . . and Jesus lifted up his eyes, and said, Father, I thank thee that thou has heard me. And I knew that thou hearest me always: but because of the people which stand by I said it, that they may believe that thou hast sent me," John 11:41–42.* Jesus intentionally prayed out loud, so the people might hear His prayer, see His answer, and then believe in Him. He rebuked the skeptics, who did not really want a sign that they might believe, but to only criticize Jesus more as they had already been doing.

The difference in honest doubt and skepticism is that skepticism has the negative state of opposition in the heart which is associated with willful rejection. A skeptic would probably have to experience a severe traumatic situation to have his eyes opened to the truth. The problem is that if the shock comes to the skeptic without someone who can to point the person to God, he may go off into alcohol, drugs, or cults.

Disbelief is a form of unbelief, but it is more through ignorance due to false teachings than in knowingly rejecting God's will or Word intentionally. Disbelief is just as serious because, in the end, the person will miss God's Will and remain in confusion, even after God has supplied the answer. Disbelief is probably very common in Christianity today. Disbelief results when we seek God and He supplies the answer in a way we did not expect or would not accept as God. The answer is then rejected as silly or ridiculous. Throughout the Scriptures God dealt with His people in dreams: Joseph in Genesis, Daniel, Solomon, Joseph, Mary, and the wise men. When God speaks to us in dreams today, the dreams are probably associated more with what was eaten the night before rather than a Word from God.

Most of we Christians have a very clear image, hard-as-a-stone, of how God should act. Any move of the Spirit in someone's life outside of our close minded image is ruled out as "emotionalism," showing off, arrogance, etc. Disbelief will result in us continually living in doubt and confusion. To try to bring comfort and stability in their beliefs, disbelievers make strict rules, many times unwritten, about how to dress and permitted activities which will ensure they are in God's will if one lives by them.

In Mark 7:6–8, Jesus talked about disbelieving, ". . . this people honoreth me with their lips, but their heart is far from me. (7)Howbeit in vain do they worship me, teaching for doctrines the commandments of men. (8)For laying aside the commandments of God, ye hold the tradition of men, as the washing of pots and cups: and many other such like things ye do." Disbelievers put aside Scriptures that talk of lifting holy hands, calling for the elders to pray when one is sick, and many other Scriptures as "not for today."

Disbelieving is also associated with our "blind side." We have done some things for so long in one particular way that we just think it has to be that way forever. In 2 Samuel 5:17–25, David found that God did things differently sometimes. The first time the Philistines came against him he inquired of the Lord and was told to fight, for he would be victorious. When very shortly after that the Philistines came against him again, God said, *(23)"Thou shalt not go up; but fetch a compass behind them, and come upon them over against the mulberry trees. (24)And let it be, when thou hearest the sound of a going in the tops of the mulberry trees, that then thou shalt bestir thyself: for then shall the Lord go out before thee, to smite the host of the Philistines."*

If David had made a rule after the first encounter with the Philistines on how to respond when he was attacked, he would have completely missed God the second time. The resulting loss of life and defeat in battle would probably have caused some to say something like, "Well, I guess it must have been God's Will for us to suffer. We did our best just like God showed us last week. I'm sure we'll learn a lot from this experience and something good will come from it." Some of David's Generals and other people probably thought it was ridiculous to wait for the sound in the mulberry trees, but David obeyed, and God provided the victory. David's confession of faith to his people was, "We must go and wait for the goings in the tops of the mulberry trees, and only then will the Lord go before us into battle."

The only way to get out of disbelief or erroneous teachings and actions is to pray and ask God to enlighten us to His Word. Read the Bible without your favorite commentary. Ask people of other beliefs what they believe, and why they believe what they believe. Most people know very little about their basic denominational beliefs. Even fewer people have Scriptural reasons why they personally believe their stated doctrines. I am not suggesting that we make an in-depth study of all the numerous religions in our country, but at least we should consider by praying and searching the Scriptures some of the main beliefs of those Christian people we meet daily in the marketplace.

Disbelief will cause us to miss so many blessings. Our blind spots are hard to identify, but we must work at opening them up to God's Word if we are to grow as Christians. Some people have decided they have enough of God to be comfortable so that any extra effort is considered unnecessary. We could say things like, "Well, maybe tongues are real for some people, but we don't have to speak in tongues to be a Christian." This expresses the attitude that we do not want anything we can get or have of God, or we do not want any more of God even if He is available. We are satisfied with what we have and are not concerned with the additional blessings God wants us to have! Our idea of growing as a Christian would be getting older and doing the same things over and over many times.

Disbelief will cause many "good" Christians to fall apart emotionally and physically when faced with serious circumstances. We might be seriously seeking God but not be receptive to the way He answers us. This is one of the reasons why so many ministers have turned to "counselors" for their own emotional needs. They have ruled out God working as He desires to in their lives because of denominational constraints.

Disbelief can result because of allowing compromise in little things until we get so confused that we do not recognize the truth when it is brought to us. Disbelief can also be due to false teaching from childhood. Many people belong to their parents' religious denomination because, "If it's good enough for Dad and dear ole Mom, it's good enough for me." Disbelief does not have the negative state of opposition of heart and willful rejection that skepticism and unbelief contain.

Disbelief is more a state of confusion caused by ignorance. The Apostle Paul says that he thanked Jesus for putting him in the ministry even after he had been a blasphemer and persecutor. Paul says in *1 Timothy 1:13, ". . . but I obtained mercy, because I did it ignorantly in unbelief."* Paul was in disbelief, a type of unbelief, but not willingly or knowingly rejecting God's Will. In fact, he thought he was serving God by trying to stamp out the "Christian cult," even though they were not called Christians at that time. When Jesus appeared to him, Paul immediately changed his beliefs and turned to serving Jesus just as vigorously as he had been persecuting the Christians. To grow in knowledge and understanding of God, we must be open to God dealing with us in ways that we have not before experienced or witnessed, like when David "had to wait for the rustling of the Mulberry trees." Therefore, we must learn to pray, communicate with God, to obtain and determine God's Pure Word because Jesus stated in *John 10:27, "My sheep hear my voice, and I know them, and they follow me,"* and in John 10:5, *"And a stranger will they not follow, but will flee from him: for they know not the voice of strangers."* We each have the responsibility to learn to seek God in prayer to be able to discern, learn, hear or whatever combination it takes to find God's Pure Word.

Unbelief is the result of a choice, made of free-will, to reject God's Will or Word. Unbelief can result from our rejecting God's Will immediately when God speaks, or from obeying to faith for a time and then turning aside in disobedient unbelief. For example, the Apostle Paul states in *1Timothy 1:5-6, "Now the end of the commandment is charity out of a pure heart, and of a good conscience, and of faith unfeigned. (6) From which some having swerved have turned aside unto vain jangling."* And in Hebrews 3:12 we read, *"Take heed, brethren, lest there be in any of you an evil heart of unbelief, in departing from the living God."* In Hebrews 3:12–19, the Scriptures point out how the children of Israel hardened their hearts and rejected God's Will for them to enter into the Promised Land because of an evil heart of unbelief.

When the Israelites sent the twelve spies into the land across the Jordan in Numbers Chapter 13, it was not to determine whether they should cross over the Jordan into the land, but they were to determine the best way to cross into the land. Ten of the spies returned and talked the people into rejecting God's Will, which they all knew was to cross over the Jordan and possess the land. The Scripture in *Hebrews 3:19 states, "So we see that they could not enter in because of unbelief."* They all knew God's Will, but they chose from an evil heart to reject it to unbelief because they did not trust that God would protect them from the giants.

The writer of Hebrews uses the example of the children of Israel failing to move into the Promised Land because of unbelief, willful rejection, to parallel or show how Christians fail to move into the rest of God, our Promised Land. Study how important it is in our daily lives to believe God and how serious it is to reject in unbelief as discussed in *Hebrews 4:1–11, "Let us therefore fear, lest, a promise being left us of entering into his rest, any of you should seem to come short of it. (2) For unto us was the gospel preached, as well as unto them: but the word preached did not profit them, not being mixed with faith in them that heard it. (3) For we which have believed do enter into rest, as He said, As I have sworn in my wrath, if they shall enter into my rest: although the works were finished from the foundation of the world. (4) For He spoke in a certain place of the seventh day from all his works. (5) And in this place again, if they shall enter into my rest. (6) Seeing therefore it remaineth that some must enter therein, and they to whom it was first preached entered not in because of unbelief: (7) Again, He limited a certain day, saying in David, Today after so long a time; as it is said, Today if ye will hear His voice, harden not your hearts. (8) For if Jesus had given them rest, then would he not afterward have spoken of another day. (9) There remaineth therefore a rest to the people of God. (10) For he that is entered into his rest, he also hath ceased from his own works, as God did from His. (11) Let us labour therefore to enter into that rest, lest any man fall after the same example of unbelief."*

    We can obey God to faith by teaching a Sunday school class for a time and then reject to unbelief by quitting the class when problems arise instead of turning to or trusting God for help. This would be like how the children of Israel would often grumble and turn aside to unbelief when they faced problems instead of continuing to trust God. Many men reject God's call to preach and then fail to enter into God's rest or peace in their hearts because of their unbelief. Many never know God's call for their lives because they refuse or just neglect to seek because they do not realize the importance of seeking or failing to seek. Knowing that we should seek and then refusing to seek is unbelief. The willful rejection of God's Will instructing us to seek Him, is unbelief. God has a special calling for each of us according to *2 Timothy 1:9, "Who hath saved us, and called us with an holy calling, not according to our works, but according to His own purpose and grace, which was given us in Christ Jesus before the world began."* And in *Ephesians 2:8–10, "For by grace are ye saved through faith; and that not of yourselves: it is the gift of God: (9) Not of works, lest any man should boast. (10) For we are his workmanship, created in Christ Jesus unto good works, which God hath before ordained that we should walk in them."* We each have a special calling, but we must seek to find it. Any church with unfilled positions of leadership in special ministries or classes needing teachers has at least that many members of the congregation in "unbelief" that are refusing God's call to those empty positions.

Lost people, non-Christians, are in a total state of unbelief until they start seeking or responding to God's Word or call to salvation. *In Titus 2:11 the Scriptures state, "For the grace of God that bringeth salvation hath appeared to all men."* Therefore, only unbelievers, those who have willfully rejected Jesus, will go to hell and be cast into the Lake of Fire. There will not be doubters in hell because God has said that He has at some time revealed the grace that brings salvation to all men. The Scriptures state we are all without excuse in *Romans 1:20, "For the invisible things of Him from the creation of the world are clearly seen, being understood by the things that are made, even His eternal power and Godhead; so that they are without excuse."* We do not see all the possible meanings or understand all the implications of how God does this for those all around the world, but He says He will. Notice in Revelation 21:8 where the people are listed that will be cast into the Lake of Fire. Unbelievers are included, but it does not mention doubters. God loves everyone so much that they will have to knowingly reject Him for them to be separated from Him for eternity in the Lake of Fire.

In Romans 1:18–32 the Scriptures state that we are all without excuse, because God has revealed Himself to everyone. But some professing themselves wise became fools and did not like to retain the knowledge of God in their minds. So, God gave them up to a reprobate mind, not knowing right from wrong. God will not send anyone to hell and the Lake of Fire by His choice! We must choose hell of our own free will. In *Isaiah 5:13–14* the Scriptures state that "*hell hath enlarged herself.*" God did not plan for mankind to reject Him because He created us to fellowship with Him. We were created to be His extension and Ambassadors here on earth. The Lake of Fire, which is often incorrectly referred to as Hell, was created for the devil and his angels, not people, as Jesus states in *Matthew 25:41, "Then shall he, the King, say also unto them on the left hand, Depart from me, ye cursed, into everlasting fire, prepared for the devil and his angels."* Many people will reject God in unbelief, but as Paul said in *Romans 3:3, "For what if some did not believe? Shall their unbelief make the faith of God without effect? God forbid: yea let God be true, but every man a liar. . . ."* Truth does not require belief; truth is truth, whether we believe it or not, as stated in *2 Timothy 2:13, "If we believe not, yet He abideth faithful: He cannot deny Himself."*

Unbelief or willful rejection could be as simple as refusing to have daily family worship, refusing to preach, refusing to teach in church, refusing to obey parents, refusing to discipline children, refusing to give up smoking, drinking or drugs, or many other problem areas that may come up daily in a Christian's life. Some of these areas seem relatively unimportant when compared to the big issues of life like, murder, rape, robbery, and congressional spending. But refusing to obey God in these "smaller" areas is causing many Christians to live sad, defeated lives in willful disobedience to the Word of God, as did the old prophet in 1 Kings 13 who disobeyed God's Word and was slain by a lion. As discussed earlier, when anyone willfully rejects God's Word, they are giving place to the devil and he will bring along as many curses of Deuteronomy Chapter 28 as he possibly can. Look around you at the Christians you know and check out the curses that match the list in Deuteronomy. Christians have become more comfortable with pills and the curses than making the effort to submit to God's Word and resist the devil. Christians are certainly not a good testimony today of God's love and blessings to our lost society of how God cares for His children in the area of health and well being.

DOUBT – SEEKING – BELIEF POINT - UNBELIEF

The simple daily issues in our lives determine our relationship with God and what we must answer for, good and bad, when we stand before Him some day. The Apostle Paul states in *Romans 14:10, "...for we shall all stand before the judgment seat of Christ."* In *2 Corinthians 5:10 the Scriptures state, "For we must all appear before the judgment seat of Christ; that every one may receive the things done in his body, according to that he hath done, whether it be good or bad."* We may be relieved and think we could not be in unbelief because we do not feel convicted in any of the above areas about God's Will. As mentioned when discussing seeking, Solomon's son "did evil because he prepared not his heart to seek the Lord." Remaining in doubt when we recognize that we are unsure of God's Will is sin and unbelief.

Christianity today is filled with doubt, skepticism, disbelief, and

CHOOSE FAITH AND GRACE
CHOOSE FAITH - DOUBT, SEEKING, BELIEF POINT, UNBELIEF

unbelief. People openly confess they are unsure about God's Will, but will not take the time to search the Scriptures to find God's Word for their situation. Others are so unsure of God's spiritual presence in daily circumstances that when they see a move of God they run or claim it is witchcraft. We all have vowed to God at salvation to serve Him, but many later refuse to respond to teach, preach, or even witness. God said in *2 Chronicles 7:14, "If my people, which are called by my name shall humble themselves, and pray, and seek my face, and turn from their wicked ways; then will I hear from heaven, and will forgive their sin, and will heal their land."* If we are to see revival and God's healing hand on our land, we all must open our hearts and minds to the truth that God is still acting and working today as in the examples He left us in the Bible. There have been only two covenants with mankind, and God would have made another covenant if He had changed the way He wanted us to relate to Him; we are under the same covenant as were the disciples and the Apostle Paul.

The unbelieving "rejecters" must renew their vows and turn back to God's call to preach, teach, and visit prisons or hospitals. This would be true revival: turning back to our vows and submitting to God's call upon our lives as Jonah did from the belly of the large fish in *Jonah 2:9, "But I will sacrifice unto thee with the voice of thanksgiving; I will pay that that I have vowed. Salvation is of the Lord."* These actions are just for people who call themselves Christians. When Christians start being honest and humbling themselves before God, lost people will be drawn to the Lord as they see God moving through His people. We Christians must set the example of living for the Lord and receiving His blessings, so that others will see and want what we have. Psalm 67 starts out like a selfish prayer, but it is not. God wants to bless us, His adopted children, so others will know how He treats His kids. *Psalm 67 states, "God be merciful unto us, and bless us; and cause His face to shine upon us; Selah. (2) That Thy way may be known upon earth, thy saving health among all nations. (3) Let the people praise thee, O God; let all the people praise thee. (4) O let the nations be glad and sing for joy: for thou shalt judge the people righteously, and govern the nations upon earth. Selah. (5) Let the people praise thee, O God; let all the people praise thee. (6) Then shall the earth yield her increase; and God, even our own God, shall bless us. (7) God shall bless us; and all the ends of the earth shall fear Him,"* and hopefully know His love and presence.

God wants to bless us so we will pass His blessings on to others. Then many others will want to turn to Him because of what they see Him doing for us. We need to recommit ourselves to God and ask Him to help us get out of any areas of doubt, skepticism, disbelief, and unbelief. Everyone around us is missing blessings because we are not the Christians we need to be in order to receive and share the blessings God wants to share through us. When we receive blessings from God, others are blessed, even though they might not recognize it as a personal blessing.

My blessings of health and a good job have kept my children from having to be concerned about my welfare. We can never be the father, mother, uncle, aunt, friend or citizen that we should be, and could be, if we are not allowing God to work in our lives as He desires. Our health care system in our country would be greatly affected if Christians would just turn and repent with all their heart to God and ask for His healing. In Mark 4:35–41, when the disciples came to Jesus fearful that the storm was going to sink their ship and they might drown, Jesus just rebuked the wind and spoke to the sea, "Peace, be still." The disciples were "blessed" with their answer; but look in verse 36. There were "other little ships" crossing with Jesus and the disciples. All of the people on the "little ships" received a blessing along with the disciples who had requested the help, and the people on the small ships did not even know who or what caused the blessing. The blessings we receive will flow out to others and they could be drawn to God as a result of our obedience.

FAITH

The only acceptable response to knowing God's Will is for us to accept His Will, regardless of what our physical senses tell us, and step out in obedience, trusting God to help us along the way as we walk by faith. Faith is the result of our choosing by free will to accept into our hearts God's Will or Word. The Scripture states in *Romans 1:17, "... The just shall live by faith," and in Hebrews 11:6, "But without faith it is impossible to please Him. ..."* Each of us, as Christians, should want to be pleasing to God. Therefore, we must live by faith. Faith is not just an option, to select or not, if we desire to serve God in His way and be pleasing to Him. The Scripture is even stronger in *Romans 14:23, which states that, ". . . whatsoever is not of faith is sin."* God will not work in and through us to others except when we are living by faith through acceptance and obedience to His Word. Remember that His Word to us is Christ, the Living Word, and God and His Word are the same as stated in *John 1:1, "In the beginning was the Word, and the Word was with God, and the Word was God."* When we fail to live by faith, we are blocking God's love to us and through us to the lives of others, and this is sin. Sin is blocking any of God's Love from entering our heart, or from us failing to share God's Love in our heart with others. Therefore, sin is blocking the flow of God's Love through us to others, or from rejecting God's Love to us for our edification or instruction. Faith is the result of acceptance of God's Will or Word into our hearts. We live from our hearts. What is accepted and stored in our hearts is what guides and motivates our actions and reactions throughout the day. We should be storing God's Word in our hearts like the Psalmist states in *Psalms 119:11, "Thy Word have I hid in mine heart, that I might not sin against thee."*

Love is related to acceptance of God's Word in *1 John 5:2–3, "By this we know that we love the children of God, when we love God, and keep His commandments (Words). For this is the love of God that we keep His commandments and His commandments (words) are not grievous."* We can see that when we fail to accept God's Will or Word into our hearts, we are blocking God's love to us and through us to others. We can only operate in love by faith. If it is not faith, it is doubt or some form of unbelief, which is not pleasing to God. Consequently, failing to live by faith will cause our growth in the Lord to stop.

We inherit the promises by faith. In *Hebrews 6:12 the Scriptures state, "That ye be not slothful, but followers of them who through faith and patience inherit the promises."* Hearing and knowing God's Word will not profit us unless we accept and respond in agreement. Jesus said in J*ohn 15:7, "If ye abide in me, and my words abide in you, ye shall ask what ye will and it shall be done unto you."* Jesus' words abiding or living in us by our choice and agreement is equivalent to praying in faith. Jesus also said in *Matthew 21:21, "Verily I say unto you, if ye have faith (Jesus' words abiding in us),*

CHOOSE FAITH AND GRACE
CHOOSE FAITH - FAITH

and doubt not, ye shall not only do this which is done to the fig tree, but also if ye shall say unto this mountain, Be thou removed, and cast into the sea, and it shall be done." For Jesus' Words to abide in us, we have to make a conscious, willful choice to receive His Words into our hearts, not just have head knowledge of His Words. When we are brought to an intellectual knowledge that something is God's Will, we must then choose to reject or accept in our hearts what we know to be true in our heads. Faith only comes when we accept God's Word in our heart that which we already know intellectually in our head.

Many people around the world know, at this instant, they need to be forgiven of their sins and that they should pray and ask God for His forgiveness. They also know they should respond to the drawing of the Spirit of God and invite the Spirit of Jesus Christ to come live in their hearts and create in them new hearts. Knowing what should be done and doing it are two different things. *Romans 10:9 states, "That if thou shalt confess with thy mouth the Lord Jesus, and shalt believe in thine heart that God hath raised him from the dead, thou shalt be saved."* Belief in-the-heart is another expression for faith. The devil has intellectual head knowledge and trembles, as stated in *James 2:19, "Thou believest that there is one God; thou doest well: the devils also believe, and tremble."* When belief is accepted and received into the heart, it brings salvation. The knowledge that all of us should ask to be forgiven and should invite Jesus into our hearts will not benefit us one bit until we willfully choose to surrender our wills and invite Jesus into our hearts. Knowing to do it and doing it are completely different and will be the deciding difference between heaven and hell for each one of us. Remember the old saying, "The road to hell is paved with good intentions!" If you have not personally asked God to forgive your sins, invited Jesus into your heart, and know He came in and changed your heart, stop reading this book right now and do it!

When we surrender our will and respond to our knowledge to invite Jesus into our heart, we receive the faith of, or for, salvation. Some might say that we must have faith first and then just place our faith in Christ for salvation. No, we have a divine knowledge of what we must do, but the instant we have faith in Christ we are saved. The same instant we receive the Spirit of Christ into our hearts, we are saved. Both happen at the same time. Paul states in *Galatians 3:26, "For we are all children of God by faith in Christ Jesus."* In

CHOOSE FAITH AND GRACE
CHOOSE FAITH - FAITH

Galatians 4:6–7, the Word says, "And because ye are sons, God hath sent forth the spirit of His Son into your hearts crying, Abba, Father. (7)Wherefore thou are no more a servant, but a son; and if a son, then an heir of God through Christ." The Spirit of God's Son Jesus Christ entering into our heart is what changes our hearts and adopts us or engrafts us into the family of God. Salvation occurs at the instant the Spirit of Christ comes into our hearts, *Romans 8:9, "But ye are not in the flesh but in the spirit, if so be that the Spirit of God dwells in you. Now if any man have not the Spirit of Christ, he is none of His."* Therefore, we cannot have faith in Christ for salvation before the Spirit of Christ enters the heart. God teaches us intellectually that we are sinners and *that Jesus is our answer, according to John 6:44–45, where Jesus said, "No man can come to me, except the Father which hath sent me draw him: and I will raise him up at the last day. (45)It is written in the prophets, And they shall be all taught of God. Every man therefore that hath heard, and hath learned of the Father, cometh unto me."* Hearing and learning are intellectual head processes that we must go through to recognize we are sinners and that Jesus is the only answer for our sin. God teaches us about sin and Jesus through His Holy Spirit, the Living Word, Christ. When we reach the intellectual truth that we must turn to Jesus for forgiveness and salvation, we either choose to accept or to reject. When we choose to accept God's Word, we will ask forgiveness and invite the Spirit of Christ into our heart. Faith comes with the acceptance of God's Will by inviting Jesus into our heart. We respond to divine knowledge, but it is not faith until we choose to accept. We could have rejected Jesus and continued in unbelief since we each have the free-will to choose either way. Until we make the choice to invite Christ into our hearts, we do not have the faith. And that which is not of faith is sin. The Scripture states in *James 1:15, "Then when lust hath conceived, it bringeth forth sin: and sin, when it is finished, bringeth forth death."*

One of the most deadly sins is to decide that it is a good idea to accept Christ to become a Christian and think someday I will, but not today. If we do not choose to receive Christ into our hearts when we come to the intellectual knowledge from God that we should, we are automatically rejecting His Spirit, Christ, to unbelief. It does not please God that we intend to accept Christ someday, a more convenient time, or when we get things straightened out. He wants us to invite and accept Christ into our hearts now, and then He will help us get things straightened out. We could not get them straightened out by ourselves anyway; the devil would not let us. After the first excuse to put Christ off, it is easier for the devil to continue to deceive a person with more excuses in the future.

Faith comes with the choice to accept God's Word, and unbelief comes with the choice to reject God's Word. Divine knowledge is what gets us to the Belief Point when we know clearly God's Living Word and that we must choose to accept or reject the Word.

Something else that is very important should be pointed out at this time. The fact that we recognized God's presence in dealing with us by His Spirit does not mean we are saved, a child of God, or born again. Jesus says in the verse above that all must be taught of God. We must recognize God and His dealing with us personally to cause us to have a desire to repent in our hearts from sin and then invite Jesus into our hearts. We may be very close to God and very knowledgeable of God, but that alone does not make us a Christian, child of God, or born again. We must pray, invite and receive the Spirit of Christ into our hearts. An example of a very good man who needed to receive Christ is in Acts Chapters 10–12. Cornelius was a devout man, feared God, gave much alms, and prayed, but was not saved until Peter came and told him about Jesus and the Spirit of Christ came into his heart in Acts 10:34–48 and Acts 11:14.

Knowledge of God and His spiritual presence thrills many who get carried away "serving God" and years later testify they missed getting saved earlier because they had not invited Jesus into their hearts. The sad part is they thought they were saved because they saw God working around them and backing up His Word when it was presented. If there will be any sadness in heaven, it will probably be when someone stands before God thinking they are a Christian and then finds out they never received Christ into their heart as Romans 8:9 states we must. The shock on the deceived person's face when he realizes he is not a Christian will only be matched by the sadness and tears in Jesus' eyes as He says depart from me to the Lake of Fire which was created for the devil and his angels, but not created for you, for I loved you every step and breath of your life.

If you are reading this and there is any doubt about the Spirit of Christ living in your heart, don't go to sleep tonight until you have prayed through to God and worked it out. Memorizing a Scripture about what you have said or done will not bring the assurance that Christ lives in your heart. Only God can clear it up for you. It is too serious to put off and decide that because of all of your good works or how good everyone thinks you are that you are probably okay. Make sure God says you are ok in some way.

Pray and get all doubt removed. Nothing on this earth is more important for you than to take the time and make sure the Spirit of Christ lives *in your heart. I believe these are the type of people talked about in Matthew 7:21–23*. These people honestly thought they were Christians and had done many wonderful works for the Lord, but Jesus will say, "*I never knew you: depart from me, ye that work iniquity.*" They never calmed down long enough to realize they had not personally accepted Jesus into their hearts. All their good works will be counted to them as "works of iniquity," simply because they were too busy and did not realize, for whatever reason, that they had not received Christ into their hearts. The wonderful works were performed by the Word of God that went forth through them, even though they were lost. God even spoke through a donkey in Numbers 22:28-30. God's Word will speak to the hearts of those who will hear, whether the speaker is a Christian or not. Therefore, we need to know that we are at peace with God in our hearts, not just witnessing God's works around us and in the lives of others.

Our first steps of faith with God are when we respond to His teaching that we are a sinner and realize we need to invite the Spirit of Jesus into our hearts. With Christ in our hearts, as joint heirs with Christ to the promises of God, we live in the "Promised Land" by faith, acceptance and obedience to God's Word. We will have to fight battles of "faith" in our Promised Land the same way Joshua and the children of Israel fought to capture their Promised Land. Just like Joshua, by faith, (acceptance and obedience to God's Word), had to conquer the enemies in his Promised Land, we will have to use our faith (acceptance and obedience to God's Word) to conquer the enemies of our Promised Land which are sin and satan.

Our relationship as an heir of God is very important to Him. In *Hebrews 6:17 the writer states, "Wherein God, willing more abundantly to show unto the heirs of promise the immutability of his counsel, confirmed it by an oath."* The Apostle Paul stated in *Romans 8:14–17, "For as many as are led by the Spirit of God, they are the sons of God. (15)For ye have not received the spirit of bondage again to fear; but ye have received the spirit of adoption, whereby we cry, Abba, Father. (16)The Spirit itself beareth witness with our spirit that we are the children of God: (17)And if children, then heirs; heirs of God and joint heirs with Christ: if so be that we suffer with Him, that we may be glorified together."* Our relationship with God, as a child of God, is very important because we only exercise the rights and enjoy the special privileges from God through faith, which results from willfully receiving His Word or Will into our hearts. God is not a respecter of persons; He respects faith, which comes from acceptance and obedience to His Word. Jesus was the Word manifested in the flesh, John 1:14. We cannot honor God and reject His Word, Christ. The Scripture states in Psalms 138:2 that God exalts His Word above all His names, and that shows why He only blesses those who accept and obey His Word, Christ.

Our walk of faith with the Lord will be affected by our self-image or by the manner in which we view our relationship with God. In *Hebrews 1:1–2, "God, who at sundry times and in divers manners spake in time past unto the fathers by the prophets, (2)Hath in these last days spoken unto us by His Son, whom He hath appointed heir of all things, by whom also He made the worlds."* Through Jesus' death and sacrifice for our sins we are made joint heirs with Jesus to all of God's promises when we receive the Spirit of Christ into our heart. In *Matthew 28:18, Jesus said, ". . . all power is given unto me in heaven and in earth."* And in *John 17:17–23, Jesus prayed for us, "Sanctify them through thy truth: thy Word is truth. (18) As thou hast sent me into the world, even so have I also sent them into the world. (19) And for their sakes I sanctify myself, that they also might be sanctified through the truth. (20) Neither pray I for these alone, but for them also which shall believe on me through their word (this includes all of us); (21) That they all may be one; as thou, Father, art in me, and I in thee, that they also may be one in us: that the world may believe that thou hast sent me. (22) And the glory which thou gavest me I have given them; that they may be one, even as we are one: (23) I in them, and thou in me, that they may be made perfect in one; and that the world may know that thou hast sent me, and hast loved them, as thou hast loved me."*

CHOOSE FAITH AND GRACE
CHOOSE FAITH - DOUBT TO FAITH

Two main points Jesus stressed in His prayer are that we might come into the oneness of the Spirit in Christ, and that as a result of this joyful relationship, others of the world might come to know Jesus.

After we have established our personal relationship with the Lord, we have a great message to share with others. *Romans 10:8 states, "But what saith it? The Word is nigh thee, even in thee, and in thy heart: that is, The Word of Faith which we preach."* As a Christian, we have a powerful message to share, a Word of Faith, acceptance and obedience to God's Word, that will bring salvation, healing and deliverance to all those who will receive the Word into their hearts. The Word or Words of Faith are the Spirit of Christ or The Living Word, Christ. When we are speaking God's Pure Words, Christ, all of the power of God is behind us, but when we add even one misplaced comma or period, the words become our words with no power, as stated before in Proverbs 30:5-6. We must seek diligently to speak God's Pure Words if we want to see God working in our circumstances. Some people will hear and reject the Word as mentioned in *Hebrews 4:2, "For unto us was the gospel preached, as well as unto them: but the Word preached did not profit them, not being mixed with faith in them that heard it."*

Our response to the gospel determines whether it becomes a curse or blessing to us. God allows us to choose, and, praise the Lord, we can choose to accept His Word to be a blessing. We do not have to reject. We can continue to accept more and more of His Word as we walk with the Lord and get to know Him better. There is never a limit placed on what we may receive from God. We can share with confidence the "Word of Faith" or "Word of Reconciliation" as the message is referred to in *2 Corinthians 5:19, "To wit, that God was in Christ, reconciling the world unto Himself, not imputing their trespasses unto them; and hath committed unto us the Word of Reconciliation."* The greatest service anyone can perform is to share the Word of Faith or Reconciliation with others. Only through faith in Jesus Christ can a heart be reconciled to God because of what God Himself did in Jesus on the cross for us.

DOUBT TO FAITH

An example of moving from doubt to faith is referred to in *Matthew 16:13–17. Jesus asked, "Whom do men say that I the Son of man am? (14)And they said, Some say that thou art John the Baptist: some, Elias; and others, Jeremias, or one of the prophets. (15)He saith unto them, But whom say ye that I am? (16)And Simon Peter answered and said, Thou art the Christ, the Son of the living God. (17)And Jesus answered and said unto him, Blessed art thou, Simon Barjona: for flesh and blood hath not revealed it unto thee, but my Father which is in heaven."* As we discussed earlier, Jesus said in J*ohn 6:45 ". . . and they shall all be taught of God. . . ."* Peter was taught of God just like each of us must be personally taught of God through His Holy Spirit, Christ. Notice also that the people were in doubt, for they had stated several possibilities as to who Jesus could have been. Peter had heard these possibilities too, but his doubt had been removed as he turned to God for guidance or the truth about Jesus. The only way for us to personally know that Jesus is the Christ is for God to personally reveal it to each of us like He did Peter. Jesus stated above in John 6:45 that we must all be taught of God, so there is no other way.

Even though Peter knew intellectually who Jesus was, he was not able to accept the Spirit of Christ into his heart as talked about in Romans 8:9, 11 and Galatians 4:6–7 until the Spirit of Jesus Christ returned on the day of Pentecost. We must remember that the new covenant, the Spirit of Christ in us, did not take effect until after Jesus' death, burial, and resurrection. *Hebrews 9:16–17 states, "For where a testament is, there must also of necessity be the death of the testator. (17) For a testament is of force after men are dead: otherwise it is of no strength at all while the testator liveth."* Peter's life before the day of Pentecost was like the other men of the Old Testament period, very strong at times and very weak at other times. After the Spirit of Christ entered his heart on the day of Pentecost, Peter became a new creature and a very strong one, being anointed by the Holy Spirit and indwelled by the Spirit of Christ.

CHOOSE FAITH AND GRACE
CHOOSE FAITH - DOUBT TO FAITH

We will remain in doubt until we start seeking and receive God's answer. God has promised if we seek with all our hearts we will find Him because then He will answer. When He answers, we must accept His answer or Word to faith, whether it appeals to our physical senses or not. When God brings us to the intellectual knowledge that we need to turn from sin and turn to Jesus, we will never be the same again, regardless of how we respond. This time in our life is often referred to as the "age of accountability," or could be referred to as the "time of accountability."

After we have faced God and know what we must do to receive God's love and forgiveness, and we then reject God's love to unbelief, our hearts will grow harder daily. Everything we see or do that causes us to think of God will harden our hearts more. Conversely, when we see Jesus as dying for our personal sins, turn to Him, and accept Jesus into our hearts, everything we are involved with throughout the day will cause us to think of God's love and prompt us to draw closer to God.

We have discussed faith as it relates to salvation. Now let's look at faith as it relates to areas of the Christian's life. It would help to list as many areas of concern as we can and then add to the list as we study through the Bible. Subject areas facing us daily that we need to know God's Will about include heaven, hell, salvation, baptism of the Holy Spirit, discipline of children, marriage relationships, Christians relating to lost people, Christians relating to Christians, abortion, activities we should or should not be involved in, types of music to listen to, places we go, church to attend, healings, clothes to wear, and many, many more areas that we will be held responsible for when we stand before God.

The first step in getting help from God is to be honest with ourselves and admit we are in doubt and need help. Expressing doubt that we are unsure of God's Will in any of the above areas is not sin, but remaining in doubt without seeking God's Will is sin. We must take the area that we are concerned about and search through the Scriptures to find what God's Word says about that subject. It might be good to start a notebook and write out Scriptures as we locate them. Then in days ahead, we will be able to review God's Word in our area of study. There are many books on the market listing Scriptures to certain problem areas. God could use one of these quick references to help or speed up locating certain Scriptures. However the method we chose to assist us in our study, we must search through God's Word and pray for understanding and wisdom. As God leads us through the Scriptures, He will be pointing out different aspects of the problem, which we must consider. Also, He will send people to us and give us more ideas. God uses sermons often to speak directly to our problems even when the pastor is unaware of the specific need. As we seek through the Scriptures, God will increase our knowledge and understanding in the area. We will eliminate many possible avenues of reactions that we will recognize as not being according to God's Word.

Suppose we were to search through the Scriptures on how we should relate to lost people. There are so many areas of concern under this one subject: our dress, our testimony, our daily conversation, our being available to go witness, and many others. We probably will never get to the point where we could rest easy and say we know exactly what we should do around lost people. However, if we are concerned enough to seek and study God's Word, we can trust that He will lead us by His Holy Spirit through witnessing situations as they develop. We may stumble some at first, but if we keep seeking and trying He will teach us how to recognize the leading of His Spirit.

There are a lot of areas of our lives and problem situations where we can know God's Will without a doubt. It would probably be easy to see that we should be studying our Bible daily and rejoicing in our hearts as mentioned in *Ephesians 5:19, which states God's Will for all of us, "Speaking to yourselves in psalms and hymns and spiritual songs, singing and making melody in your heart to the Lord."* Whether we are seeking to live that way and can actually see improvement in our lives by our joyfulness increasing will determine if we are accepting Ephesians 5:19 into our hearts to faith or not. If we are walking by faith according to Ephesians 5:17–19, every time we recognize our thoughts have drifted from the Lord and are involved in idle imaginations, we will take control of those thoughts and set them back on the Scriptures or on a melody of praise. We have to make the effort to take control of our thoughts and emotions to direct or set them on the things of God.

CHOOSE FAITH AND GRACE
CHOOSE FAITH - DOUBT TO FAITH

Our greatest battle with the devil is in our minds. We need to seek God's Will and have His Word in our hearts, so when the devil attacks, we can put up our Shield of Faith and then let the Living Words, Christ, which we accepted in our hearts as our Shield of Faith, actually fight our battle for us. That is really great! We have a shield that not only protects us but fights our battles, too. The Apostle Paul stated in *2 Corinthians 10:3–5, "For though we walk in the flesh, we do not war after the flesh: (4) (For the weapons of our warfare are not carnal, but mighty through God to the pulling down of strongholds:) (5) Casting down imaginations, and every high thing that exalteth itself against the knowledge of God, and bringing into captivity every thought to the obedience of Christ. . . ."*

To fight the devil and win in our minds, we must have knowledge of God and His Word in our hearts for the area of attack, and then we must submit to God's Word in that area. We will not win if we fight and argue when we know it is God's will for us to pray. *Psalm 109:4 says, "For my love they are my adversaries: but I give myself to prayer."* And in *Matthew 5:44, Jesus said, "Love your enemies, bless them that curse you, do good to them that hate you, and pray for them which despitefully use you and persecute you. . . ."* It is a lot easier to say than to do, but we must try while praying for God's help to obey His Word and pray for our "enemies" that they might be set free of the devil's clutches which allowed the devil to work his evil through them to harm us. The only way to get a victory is to pray that the persons involved be delivered from the deceit of the devil because he is the enemy not the people. If they had been under God's leadership, they would not have done the harmful things to us.

The only way for us to obtain victory when the devil attacks our thoughts is to bring forth the Scripture, the Living Word, Christ, that deals with the subject and then have the support of agreement with the Scripture in our hearts. If in our hearts we do not believe the Scripture or do not accept it, then we will lose the battle in our heads. Even if we quote the Scripture over and over against the devil, he and God both will know we do not mean it. For example, we may say along with *Psalm 37:25, ". . . I have not seen the righteous forsaken, nor his seed begging bread."* But in our hearts we could be saying, "Where's God now? Why did He let me get in this mess if He's concerned and is still going to help me?" The devil will hear our confessions and know we do not believe or have the Word in our hearts.

If we believe *Philippians 4:13, "I can do all things through Christ which strengtheneth me,"* we should not be afraid to teach a Sunday school class, lead a devotional, or even go inside a jail to visit. We could sing, "Red and yellow, black and white; they are precious in His sight, . . ." but just do not let them come to our church. "Victory in Jesus" will only come when we receive the knowledge of God's Word from our heads into our hearts and then allow the Word, Christ, to control us from our hearts. Our daily walk of faith with the Lord is just a bunch of reactions to simple situations, as mentioned above. In some of the situations, we can clearly know God's Will. In others, we trust that He will lead us through them as we go.

A preacher can often know what sermon to preach long before he arrives at church. We can know God's Will about which class to attend, which job to take, which house to buy, etc. With family problems, we know clearly it is God's Will to pray together and seek God's Will, but we may not have a clear answer as to what God's specific solution is. It may take time and some changes for each member of the family; perhaps none would have understood the solution if it had been given immediately after the first prayer. But, we must receive God's promise into our heart that tells us if we seek with all our heart, He will hear and answer. Then we must keep seeking in obedience and faith until we receive His answer. Giving up and deciding it is causing too much trouble or that it "just must not be God's Will for us to be together" is turning from faith in God's promises to unbelief.

The Scriptures say that Abraham was strong in faith, being fully persuaded that what God had promised He was able and would perform. In *Romans 4:20 Paul stated, "He staggered not at the promise of God through unbelief; but was strong in faith, giving glory to God."* For us to grow in faith, we must begin by living the simple life of God's Will that we already know: studying God's Word, helping neighbors, being honest in daily activities, forgiving those who have wronged us, and serving God by some means of confessing our faith in Jesus Christ to the lost world.

CHOOSE FAITH AND GRACE
CHOOSE FAITH - HOPE, DOUBT, SEEKING, BELIEF, TRUST, FAITH, AND WALKING BY FAITH

When we commit our lives to the Lord, we are promising Him to live according to His way by obeying His Word. The only way we will know His way is to seek Him through His Word. It is difficult to seek through the Scriptures to find God's Will about some serious circumstances when it seems that the world is caving in on us. We must take the time when things are relatively calm for in-depth study, seeking God's Will about areas that we are fairly certain we will face in the future. Areas of concern may include marriage, death of loved ones, healing, spiritual gifts, service for God, etc. It helps to know ahead of time what God's Word says in different areas of our lives so we can stand in faith against problems that we encounter.

HOPE, DOUBT, SEEKING, BELIEF, TRUST, FAITH, AND WALKING BY FAITH

The Biblical relationships between hope, doubt, seeking, belief point, faith, and walking by faith can be clearly demonstrated as we analyze the story of King Jehoshaphat in 2 Chronicles 20:1-26. The Scriptures will come alive to you as you see how the above words are related and your Bible studies will become exciting.

Jehoshaphat, in 2 Chronicles 20:1-28, feared when told he was surrounded by three armies, verses 1-3. Remember though, fear is not the problem; it is the symptom of the problem which is doubt. Jehoshaphat feared because he did not know what to do about the armies; he was in doubt, but he knew what to do to get out of doubt. Jehoshaphat set himself to seek the Lord for guidance, verses 3-13, he received God's Rhema, Living Word, for the situation, verses 14-17, he then accepted God's Word, verses 18-19, he "walked-by-faith to obey God's Word, verses 20-22, and then he received God's total victory with the accompanying rewards, 22-28.

The story begins in *2 Chronicles 20:1-3 which states, "It came to pass after this also, that the children of Moab, and the children of Ammon, and with them other beside the Ammonites, came against Jehoshaphat to battle. (2) Then there came some that told Jehoshaphat, saying There cometh a great multitude against thee from beyond the sea on this side*

Syria; and, behold, they be in Hazazontamar, which is Engedi. (3) And Jehoshaphat feared, and set himself to seek the Lord, and proclaimed a fast throughout all Judah."

The first three verses show that King Jehoshaphat is faced with a serious problem, so serious that he had fear. Fear is a symptom of Jehoshaphat's problem; the problem he is suddenly faced with is doubt as to what to do about the armies that surround him.

When we have doubt in a serious situation, either because we do not know what God wants us to do or we are unaware of God's presence, the devil will try to take advantage of us by tormenting us with what we call fear, but it is actually the spirit of the devil. The Scripture says in 2 Timothy 1:7 that fear is a spirit, and that God has not given us the spirit of fear, but of love, power and a sound mind. The more we give in to the fear (devil), the less likely we will be able to find God's Word or Will for the situation, and the devil will have more advantage or ability to harm us. When we are faced with any situation in which we do not know how to respond, we should do as Jehoshaphat did and set ourselves to seek the Lord. As discussed in previous chapters, seeking can include many different activities, such as studying the Scriptures, praying, fasting, and obtaining Christian advice.

Jehoshaphat proclaimed a fast as part of his seeking God. Remember that fasting is not just giving up something, but giving up something very important to us that we like or use frequently. Every time we think of what we have given up, we must pray about the purpose of the fast, instead of responding as we normally would. Depending on what we give up for our fast and how much it is a part of our life, we may wind up praying continually. When we fast from food, every time we think of food in any way, we pray about our problem. Jehoshaphat not only fasted but also declared a fast for everyone throughout the land.

When Jehoshaphat heard that the three armies surrounded him, immediately a hope was developed. His hope was naturally for deliverance from the armies. He trusted God enough to turn to Him for help in this time of trouble. So from the beginning, Jehoshaphat placed his hope for deliverance in God and trusted that God would provide a way. From his relationship with God, Jehoshaphat knew he could trust God. At this point, Jehoshaphat's trust in God became the substance of his hope. If he had not trusted God, he probably would have placed his hope in obtaining help from some other source, as did King Asa in 2 Chronicles 6:7, when he turned to the king of Syria for help. Jehoshaphat's hope, his desired outcome, was for a deliverance from the three armies, and he placed his hope in God because he trusted that God would provide a way for victory, even though at this time he had no idea as to how the victory would be achieved.

Second Chronicles 20:4 – 13 states, "And Judah gathered themselves together, to ask help of the Lord: even out of all the cities of Judah they came to seek the Lord. (5) And Jehoshaphat stood in the congregation of Judah and Jerusalem, in the house of the Lord, before the new court, (6) And said, O Lord God of our fathers, art not thou God in heaven? And rulest not thou over all the kingdoms of the heathen? And in thine hand is there not power and might, so that none is able to withstand thee? (7) Art not thou our God, who didst drive out the inhabitants of this land before thy people Israel, and gavest it to the seed of Abraham thy friend forever? (8) And they dwelt therein, and have built thee a sanctuary therein for thy name, saying, (9) If, when evil cometh upon us, as the sword, judgment, or pestilence, or famine, we stand before this house, and in thy presence, (for thy name is in this house,) and cry unto thee in our affliction, then thou wilt hear and help. (10) And now, behold, the children of Ammon and Moab and mount Seir, whom thou wouldest not let Israel invade, when they came out of the land of Egypt, but they turned from them, and destroyed them not; (11) Behold, I say, how they reward us, to come to cast us out of thy possession, which thou hast given us to inherit. (12) O our God, wilt thou not judge them? For we have no might against this great company that cometh against us; neither know we what to do: but our eyes are upon thee. (13) And all Judah stood before the Lord, with their little ones, their wives, and their children."

Jehoshaphat and all Judah came before the temple and fasted in response to the written Word that he had as a promise from God. God made this promise to Solomon at the dedication of the new temple in 1 Kings 8 and

CHOOSE FAITH AND GRACE
CHOOSE FAITH - HOPE, DOUBTR SEEKING, BELIEF, TRUST, FAITH, AND WALKING BY FAITH

2 Chronicles Chapters 6 and 7. God stated in the written promise that if the children of Israel would humble themselves, come before the temple and call out to Him when famine, pestilence, enemy, or any other problem came upon them, He would hear and deliver them from their problem.

Jehoshaphat knew this written promise, believed the promise, and accepted it to faith. Because of his trust in God and faith in the written promise guiding him, he called all the people together before the temple during the fast to call out to God as instructed. At the end of Jehoshaphat's prayer, he states that they have no might against this large army, and neither do they know how to respond except to turn their eyes to God. They did not know specifically how to deal with the armies, but they did know what to do to find God's guidance: turn to the Lord and gather before the temple. So when we do not know how to respond, we should also turn to the Lord for His Living Word for guidance. The Psalmist states in *Psalms 119:105, "Thy Word is a lamp unto my feet, and a light unto my path."* The written Word told Jehoshaphat to go before the temple and call out to God. They did all they knew from the written Word; then they left it in God's hands for a response.

In Deuteronomy 2:4,9,19, the Scripture says that these three armies were the descendents of Esau and Lot's two daughters. God had given each of these three countries an inheritance. God had given them victory over giants to capture their lands, and He had protected them from the children of Israel when they came out of bondage and passed through their territory in Deuteronomy 2:2-23. Now, these nations who had been blessed by God were coming against His chosen people. God's promise to Abraham in *Genesis 12:3 was, "I will bless them that bless thee, and curse him that curseth thee..."* This promise was passed down through the generations to God's people. Now we will understand why God came against these armies so harshly in His answer to Jehoshaphat in the next few verses.

"Then upon Jahaziel (the son of Zechariah, the son of Benaiah, the son of Jeiel, the son of Mattaniah,) a Levite of the sons of Asaph, came the Spirit of the Lord in the midst of the congregation; (15) And he said, Hearken ye, all Judah, and ye inhabitants of Jerusalem, and thou King Jehoshaphat, Thus saith the Lord unto you, Be not afraid nor dismayed by reason of this

great multitude; for the battle is not yours, but God's. (16) Tomorrow go ye down against them: behold, they come up by the cliff of Ziz; and ye shall find them at the end of the brook, before the wilderness of Jeruel. (17) Ye shall not need to fight in this battle: set yourselves, stand ye still, and see the salvation of the Lord with you, O Judah and Jerusalem: fear not, nor be dismayed; tomorrow go out against them: for the Lord will be with you," 2 Chronicles 20:14-17.

The Spirit of the Lord came upon Jahaziel and spoke the Rhema Word, Christ, to Jehoshaphat and the entire congregation. Now that they had received God's Word for what to do next, they had to choose to accept His Word to faith or reject His Word to unbelief. Jehoshaphat is at the Belief Point, He has heard God's Living Word, Christ, and is completely out of doubt because God has told him exactly what to do. Now their trust was tested. Did they trust God enough to actually accept His Words to faith and march out of the gates without weapons before three armies while singing praises as they went? The lives of all the men, women and children were on the line. They would all die when they marched out the gates, if what Jahaziel said was not really from God. They would have just as big a problem if they believed what Jahaziel said was from God, but they were afraid and did not trust God enough to accept and obey what God had said.

When the children of Israel came out of Egypt and reached the Jordan River, they all knew it was God's will to cross over, but they did not trust God to deliver them from the giants and were afraid because of the report of the ten spies (Hebrews 3:12, 19). All the men ages twenty and older, except Caleb and Joshua, perished in the wilderness because they did not trust God enough to obey His Will and enter the land. So, just knowing God's Word does not make it automatically easy for us to accept His Word in all circumstances. This is where trust is introduced. Do we trust God enough to accept His Word to faith, even when it sounds silly or ridiculous, like marching out the gates without weapons before three armies singing praises? That would certainly not be a war council's logical decision as to what to do with three armies surrounding our country.

Jehoshaphat's response is given in *2 Chronicles 20:18-19,* "And

CHOOSE FAITH AND GRACE
CHOOSE FAITH - HOPE, DOUBT SEEKING, BELIEF, TRUST, FAITH, AND WALKING BY FAITH

Jehoshaphat bowed his head with his face to the ground: and all Judah and the inhabitants of Jerusalem fell before the Lord, worshipping the Lord. (19) And the Levites, of the children of the Kohathites, and of the children of the Korhites, stood up to praise the Lord God of Israel with a loud voice on high."

Jehoshaphat and the congregation accepted the "words" through Jahaziel as God speaking to them. They immediately bowed their heads and worshipped the Lord for His answer on how to handle the three armies. They trusted God enough to accept His Word to faith. Now their hope, desired deliverance, was based on faith, the acceptance of God's Word through Jahaziel. Now faith, their acceptance of God's Word, was the substance of their hope, which is still to be delivered from the three armies. God's Word was the substance of their faith; therefore, their hope is now based on their faith, which is based on their acceptance of and obedience to God's Word. Now to receive deliverance, which is their hope, they must accept and obey completely God's Word to march out of the gates and set themselves before the three armies.

At this point, Jehoshaphat's situation and response is a good example of what it means to "claim-something-by-faith" or make a "confession-of-faith." Now that God had spoken to them the Rhema Living Word, Christ, about what they were to do in the situation, their "confession-of-faith" was exactly what God said, no more or no less. When the armies came against Jehoshaphat, he didn't start running around "claiming-by-faith" that God was going to move his mountain as in Mark 11:23, which in this case would be the three armies. He didn't stand on the walls or at the gate and speak, "Armies move in the name of God!" as many "faith" teachers would have us do. Jehoshaphat sought God for His Will or Word. God said in 2 Chronicles 20:15-17, the battle was His, for them to set themselves and see the victory. Now Jehoshaphat and the congregation all had a "confession-of-faith" and could "claim-the-victory-by-faith," but only if they responded to God's Word properly and marched out of the gates like God told them. They had to not only mentally accept God's Word, but also they had to march out of the gates unarmed before three armies to complete their part of the "claiming-the-victor-by-faith." From the time God spoke to them, they had to "walk-by-faith" while "claiming-the-victory-by-faith" that afternoon, night and the next morning before they actually marched out the gates.

CHOOSE FAITH AND GRACE
CHOOSE FAITH - HOPE, DOUBT, SEEKING, BELIEF, TRUST, FAITH, AND WALKING BY FAITH

Their "confession-of-faith" was to confess only what God had told them, the Rhema Living Word, about their problem to get them out of doubt. Now if they accept and obey to faith what God has told them, they can then "claim-by-faith" the victory or fulfillment of their hope, the desired victory in God's manner or method. Their confession of faith must be His Pure Words that He spoke to them, or He will not back up their confession and they will be made a liar and be defeated, *Proverbs 30:5-6, "Every Word of God is pure: He is a shield unto them that put their trust in Him. (6) Add thou not unto His Words, lest He reprove thee, and thou be found a liar.".*

Jehoshaphat feared when he heard about the three armies. He set himself to seek the Lord, followed the written Word available to him, and humbled himself before the Lord. Then God spoke to him the Rhema Word of faith, Romans 10:8. Now Jehoshaphat and the people are walking-by-faith, in acceptance and obedience to God's Word.

The Scripture tells of their early morning preparation in *2 Chronicles 20:20, "And they rose early in the morning, and went forth into the wilderness of Tekoa: and as they went forth, Jehoshaphat stood and said, 'Hear me, O Judah, and ye inhabitants of Jerusalem; Believe in the Lord your God, so shall ye be established; believe his prophets, so shall ye prosper.'"*

After a night's sleep, Jehoshaphat gives the men a pep talk and encourages them in their faith, their commitment to accepting and obeying God's Word, which they had made the previous day. Now all that is left for Jehoshaphat and the men to do is march out of the gates as God instructed. It sounds simple reading about it, but with three armies waiting to kill them many of the people probably had a rush of adrenaline when they started out of the gates unarmed.

God did not tell them how to march out of the gates, so they made specific plans in *2 Chronicles 20:21, "And when he had consulted with the people, he appointed singers unto the Lord, and that should praise the beauty of holiness, as they went out before the army, and to say, Praise the Lord, for His mercy, endureth for ever."*

CHOOSE FAITH AND GRACE
CHOOSE FAITH - HOPE, DOUBT, SEEKING, BELIEF, TRUST, FAITH, AND WALKING BY FAITH

The preparations were complete, and they knew what to do. The time has come now that they must march out the gates before the three armies. The Scriptures state in *2 Chronicles 20:22-25, "And when they began to sing and to praise, the Lord set ambushments against the children of Ammon, Moab, and mount Seir, which were come against Judah; and they were smitten. (23) For the children of Ammon and Moab stood up against the inhabitants of mount Seir, utterly to slay and destroy them: and when they had made an end of the inhabitants of Seir, every one helped to destroy another. (24) And when Judah came toward the watch tower in the wilderness, they looked unto the multitude, and, behold, they were dead bodies fallen to the earth, and none escaped. (25) And when Jehoshaphat and his people came to take away the spoil of them, they found among them in abundance both riches with the dead bodies, and precious jewels, which they stripped off for themselves, more than they could carry away: and they were three days in gathering of the spoil, it was so much."* Notice that after they began to sing and praise, then the Lord set the ambush against the enemy. After we do all God asks us to do, then He will do all He said He would do. Jehoshaphat's hope, deliverance from the three armies, was fulfilled by his faith, acceptance and obedience to God's Word. Our victory over the things of the world, 1 John 5:4, is through our faith, acceptance and obedience to God's Word. After the three days of gathering the spoils of the "battle," Jehoshaphat gathered everyone the next day for a praise and worship service, stated in *2 Chronicles 20:26, "And on the fourth day they assembled themselves in the valley of Berachah; for there they blessed the Lord:"*

Hope is our desired outcome, or victory, for our problem or circumstances. Trust is based on our relationship with God. Trust is developed with people or God by daily fellowshipping with them and getting to personally know their character. Trust is based on our relationship with God, and faith comes from hearing and accepting God's Word; they are related but very different. Our trust in God gives us the courage to accept God's Word when He asks us to march out before three armies or the devil without physical weapons. When a problem comes in our life, if we at first do not know God's Will or Rhema Living Word, our hope will be based on our trust in God, and the best we can determine to do from the written Word. As we seek God about our problem and He speaks the Rhema Living Word to us, we must have the courage to trust God enough to accept what He has said to faith. If we accept what God has said, then our hope will be based on our newly received faith, acceptance and obedience to the Rhema Living Word God has spoken to us about our problem.

God's Word is the substance of our faith, and our faith is the substance of our hope. Therefore, God's Word is the substance of our hope when we accept and obey God's Word to faith. The Psalmist in *Psalms 119:147 writes, "I prevented the dawning of the morning, and cried: I hoped in Thy Word."* Also, the Rhema Living Word, Christ, that God spoke to us about our problem is the exact pure confession-of-faith that will cause our "mountain" to move as spoken of in Mark 11:23. We cannot just make up a good sounding positive confession, find several Scriptures to back up the confession, and then expect God to jump through hoops to perform for us. We must seek Him for the Living Word to get us out of doubt and find out what He wants us to confess, and then He will back up His Living Word He gave us when we confess "it." If we obey His Word, God fights the battles, we receive the blessings, and He receives the praise.

JESUS' FAITH

Several Scriptures refer to "the faith of Jesus," "the faith of Christ," or "the faith of the Son of God." Without the proper understanding of these Scriptures, it might appear that there is a faith greater than our faith that we should seek, and that our faith might not be enough for every situation. First, let us take a look at Jesus' faith to see what "Jesus' faith" means.

Faith is always the result of accepting and obeying God's Will or Word. Regardless of how God reveals His Word or Will, or how we come to understand His Word or Will, we must accept His Word to faith or reject to unbelief. Jesus came to show us the way; to show us the perfect walk of obedience to faith.

In John 5:19, Jesus said of Himself, "Verily, Verily, I say unto you, The Son can do nothing of Himself, but what He seeth the Father do; for what things soever He doeth, these also doeth the Son likewise." And in *John 5:30, Jesus said, "I can of mine own self do nothing: as I hear, I judge:*

and my judgment is just; because I seek not mine own will, but the will of the Father which hath sent me." In *John 8:28–29, Jesus said, "When ye have lifted up the Son of man, then shall ye know that I am He, and that I do nothing of myself; but as my Father hath taught me, I speak these things. (29) And He that sent me is with me: the Father hath not left me alone; for I do always those things that please Him."*

Jesus said He does only what He sees the Father do, seeks only His Father's will, can do nothing of Himself, and does only what His Father taught Him. His Father is always with Him, so He always does those things which please His Father.

This was the perfect walk of faith, accepting His Father's will and doing only what He was told; therefore, He always pleased His Father. Jesus stated in *John 10:17–18, Matthew 26:39,42 and Luke 22:42* that He did not have to give His life for us, but He chose to give His life for us in agreement with His Father's will, "*Therefore doth my Father love me, because I lay down my life, that I might take it again. (18) No man taketh it from me, but I lay it down of myself. I have power to lay it down, and I have power to take it again. This commandment have I received of my Father."* In *Matthew 26 and Luke 22, Jesus praying in Gethsemane said, "O My father, if it be possible, let this cup pass from me: nevertheless not as I will, but as thou wilt"* and then, *"O my Father, if this cup may not pass away from me, except I drink it, thy will be done."* Jesus accepted His Father's Will to faith and gave His life for us in death on the cross.

In *Romans 5:19,* speaking of Adam and Jesus, the Scripture states, "*For as by one man's disobedience many were made sinners, so by the obedience of One shall many be made righteous."* And in *Philippians 2:7–11* the Scripture states of Jesus, *"But made Himself (Jesus) of no reputation, and took upon Him the form of a servant, and was made in the likeness of men: (8)And being found in fashion as a man, He humbled Himself, and became obedient unto death, even the death of the cross. (9)Wherefore God also hath highly exalted Him, and given Him a name which is above every name: (10)That at the name of Jesus every knee should bow, of things in heaven, and things in earth, and things under the earth; (11)And that every tongue should confess that Jesus Christ is Lord, to the glory of God the Father."*

Because Jesus accepted His Father's Word or Will to faith and became obedient unto death, God exalted His name above all names. That is why we must humble ourselves and call out to Jesus for salvation. Also, because of Jesus' perfect walk of faith and obedience, the Father has committed all judgment unto the Son. *John 5:22–23 states, "For the Father judgeth no man, but hath committed all judgment unto the Son: (23) That all men should honour the Son, even as they honour the Father. He that honoureth not the Son honoureth not the Father which hath sent Him."* In *Romans 8:9 the Scriptures state, "…now if any man have not the Spirit of Christ, he is none of His."* Everyone is God's creation, and God loves everyone with a perfect love, but only those who receive the Spirit of Christ into their heart are adopted into His family as His children.

Hebrews 2:17–18 and Hebrews 4:15 state that Jesus was tempted in all things as we are, *"Wherefore in all things it behooved Him to be made like unto His brethren, that He might be a merciful and faithful high priest in things pertaining to God, to make reconciliation for the sins of the people. (18) For in that He Himself hath suffered being tempted, He is able to succour them that are tempted,"* and *"…but was in all points tempted like as we are, yet without sin."* In all these temptations, Jesus chose His Father's Will or Word to faith and did not sin. In *Hebrews 5:7–9* the Scripture states about Jesus, *"Who in the days of His flesh, when He had offered up prayers and supplications with strong crying and tears unto Him (God) that was able to save Him (Jesus) from death, and was heard in that He feared; (8)Though He were a Son, yet learned Heobedience by the things which He suffered; (9) And being made perfect, He became the author of eternal salvation unto all them that obey Him."* Notice the last phrase states eternal salvation to those of us who obey Him. The Scripture states in *Hebrews 12:2, "Looking unto Jesus the author and finisher of our faith; who for the joy that was set before Him endured the cross, despising the shame, and is set down at the right hand of the throne of God."* Jesus is the author of our faith; He wrote the book of the perfect walk of faith. He accepted His Father's Word and Will in perfect obedience to faith without sin all the way to the cross. Jesus looked through the cross and saw His victory over death, and how His Spirit would come back to live in mankind's hearts. Jesus willingly became the perfect sacrifice for our sin debt, so that those who turn to Him could be forgiven and set free of their sin debt.

Jesus had to die to seal the new covenant. *Hebrews 9:16 reads, "For where a testament is, there must also of necessity be the death of the testator. For a testament is of force after men are dead; otherwise it is of no strength at all while the testator liveth."* A testament or will is in effect only after men die; it can be changed at any time until death. After death, the will is set into force and cannot be changed.

Jesus' faith, perfect obedience to His Father's Will and Word, provided the example and became the perfect sacrifice on the cross for our sins to be forgiven, but only if we turn to Him and ask for forgiveness. Jesus did not forgive all of our sins on the cross; He fulfilled the requirements for all our sins to be forgiven when we humble ourselves and ask forgiveness. If Jesus had forgiven all our sins on the cross, everyone would be born as a totally forgiven Christian, and everyone would go to heaven automatically. Jesus' faith made the provision for our salvation, but it is our faith, i.e., acceptance and obedience to God's Word which leads us to salvation and to become a child of God. Ephesians 2:8 states, "For by grace are ye saved through faith; and that not of yourselves; it is the gift of God." Our faith is a result of our acceptance of God's Word that we are sinners, that Jesus is the only answer for our sins, that we must humble ourselves and ask His forgiveness of our sins, and that we must invite the Spirit of Christ into our hearts. Only after we have actually asked forgiveness and invited the Spirit of Christ into our heart will we receive the grace, the Spirit of Christ, into our hearts for salvation. When God sends the Spirit of His Son into our heart, we are born again, become a child of God, receive the new heart, are saved from our sins, and we are joint heirs with Jesus as stated in *Galatians 4:6-7, "And because ye are sons, God hath sent forth the Spirit of His Son into your hearts, crying, Abba, Father. (7) Wherefore thou art no more a servant, but a son; and if a son, then an heir of God through Christ."* All of these changes happen the instant we receive the Spirit of God's Son, Christ, into our heart.

Choose Faith and Grace
Choose Faith - Jesus' Faith

Our faith is spoken of in the Scriptures several times. In Romans 5:1 and Galatians 3:8 the Scriptures state we are justified, or set free of our sins, by our faith, which is our acceptance and obedience to God's Word. Galatians 3:26 states we are all children of God by our faith, our acceptance and obedience to God's Word. Our faith, our acceptance and obedience to God's Word, is our shield against the fiery darts of the wicked, so states Ephesians 6:16. Our faith, acceptance and obedience to God's Word, is the breastplate which protects us from attacks of the wicked one in 1 Thessalonians 5:8. We inherit the "great and precious promises" of God not just by being a Christian, but by our faith, our believing, accepting and obeying God's promises which He double sealed to us in Hebrews 6:13-18.

Christians can have faith and receive salvation but disbelieve some of the great promises, and thereby miss out on the promises that could be fulfilled in their lives for their health, protection, and everyday joy of fellowship. The Scripture states in Hebrews 11:6 that the only way we can please God is through our faith, our believing, accepting and obeying God's Word or Will, and any rejection of God's Word or Will is SIN, as stated in *Romans 14:23, ". . . for whatsoever is not of faith is sin."* Jesus' faith made provision for our new relationship with God in the new covenant, but it is our faith that we must live by daily. The Scripture states in 1 John 5:4, ". . . and this is the victory that overcometh the world, even our faith."

Jesus lived by His faith; We live by our faith. Our walk of faith under the new covenant with God is made possible only because of Jesus' perfect walk of faith before us. In *Galatians 2:20, the Apostle Paul makes that kind of comment when he says, "...the life which I now live in the flesh I live by the faith of the Son of God, who loved me, and gave Himself for me,"* and in E*phesians 3:12, ". . . in whom we have boldness and access with confidence by the faith of Him."* Because of what Jesus did for us and the relationship He had with His Father, we can have boldness and access to God with confidence as we accept and obey God's Word like Jesus did because we are joint heirs with Jesus.

The only way we can have the same faith of Jesus, is for us to accept God's Word or Will and obey the same as Jesus did. We have the same option to accept and obey God's Word as Jesus did. The choices we make are ours. We must, of our own free-will, choose to accept God's Word to faith or reject His Word to unbelief. Just because we are Christians does not mean we are walking-by-faith in our daily lives. We must make all of our choices in obedience to God's Word to walk perfectly by faith daily, as Jesus made all of His choices and walked daily by faith.

When Jesus came to John the Baptist in *John 1:29, John said, ". . . behold the Lamb of God, which taketh away the sin of the world."* Because of Jesus' perfect, sinless walk-of-faith, He became our "lamb without blemish" to be offered as a perfect sacrifice to pay the price for our sin debt. Peter stated in *1 Peter 1:18–19, "Forasmuch as ye know that ye were not redeemed with corruptible things, as silver and gold, from your vain conversation received by tradition from your fathers; (19)But with the precious blood of Christ, as of a lamb without blemish and without spot."* Jesus paid the price for our sins to be forgiven and He walked the perfect daily walk of faith in accepting and obeying all of His Father's Word. We each must seek daily to make our decisions in accordance with God's Will and Word as Jesus did for us to be walking by faith as Jesus walked.

Our Christian society has many different beliefs about what faith is, how to "activate" our faith, how to "release" faith, how to operate faith, measures of faith, and so forth. In the following material I will discuss several of the commonly broadcast errors being taught about faith.

MEASURE OF FAITH

We receive faith by our accepting and obeying God's Living Word, Christ, when we hear His Word. Jesus says in *John 6:63, "…the Words that I speak unto you, they are Spirit, and they are life."* When we recognize that God is speaking to us and we accept His Words; we are receiving His Spirit, Christ the Living Word, into our heart, and we are receiving the Love of the Word or Spirit into our heart. It is possible to hear intellectually the Words God is speaking to us and then reject the Love of the Word or Spirit of the Words, Christ, from our hearts as stated in *2 Thessalonians 2:10, "And with all deceivableness of unrighteousness in them that perish; because they received not the Love of the truth, that they might be saved."* They heard God's Word, the Truth, but did not accept and receive the Spirit of the Words into their hearts. The same result of failing to accept and receive the Spirit of God's Words to faith is given in *Hebrews 4:2, "For unto us was the gospel preached, as well as unto them: but the Word preached did not profit them, not being mixed with faith in them that heard it."* They heard the Word of the gospel, Truth, but did not accept and receive the Spirit or Love of the Word into their hearts.

As we grow from childhood and start recognizing God speaking to us, we must make a choice each time to accept or reject the Spirit of the Words, Christ. Each time we accept, we are growing in faith by a measure. The measures may be large or small depending on how God evaluates them. For our purpose as we try to be pleasing to God, the Apostle Paul states in *Romans 14:24. "... for whatsoever is not of faith is sin."* If we reject any of God's Word, we have failed to receive the Love of the Words, Christ, that He spoke to us and we are in unbelief for that situation.

Jesus states in *John 6:45, "It is written in the prophets, And they shall be all taught of God. Every man therefore that hath heard, and hath learned of the Father, cometh unto me."* Some of the first things God will probably start teaching young people is that He loves them, that they are sinners, that Jesus is the answer for their sins, that they must humble themselves and call out to Him for the salvation available to them. If when God tells someone they are a sinner and they reject it, they cannot be "saved" or come to Jesus because they are not "hearing and learning of the Father" as Jesus said above, and they are not receiving the measure of faith for those Words that God spoke to them. If the person accepts he is a sinner, he receives the measure of faith for those Words from God and continues on to more of God's teaching. God will then teach the "sinner" that His Son Jesus has provided the solution for his sins, as in *Romans 6:23, "For the wages of sin is death; but the gift of God is eternal life through Jesus Christ our Lord."* Some people who have accepted that they are a sinner to faith may stumble at Jesus being the answer for their sin and reject becoming a "Jesus freak." They have not received the Love of these Words, Christ, that God has spoken to them or the measure of faith for this part of God's teaching, and they cannot be "saved" as long as they continue to reject to unbelief that Jesus is the answer for their sin. For those who accept they are a sinner and that Jesus is the answer for their sin, God will tell them they need to humble themselves, surrender their lives to Him, ask His forgiveness and invite His Spirit, Christ, into their hearts. Each of these teachings by God must be accepted or responded to positively for each individual to continue to grow in measures of faith. A person on skid-row or in a fox-hole may include all of these steps in one whole hearted cry of "Help" to God because God hears and answers heart language as stated in *2 Corinthians 3:16, "Nevertheless when it (the heart) shall turn to the Lord, the vail shall be taken away."* And God also says in Isaiah 45:22, "Look unto me, and be ye saved, all the ends of the earth: for I am God, and there is none else."

Once a person has properly met God's criteria for salvation, or the acceptable responses to God's teaching to faith, they will have – "the measure of faith"- for salvation. In other words, as Jesus said in John 6:45 they have heard, learned of the Father, and have come to me, Jesus. At that time God responds as stated in *Galatians 4:6-7, "And because ye are sons, God hath sent forth the Spirit of His Son into your hearts, crying, Abba, Father. (7) Wherefore thou art no more a servant, but a son; and if a son, then an heir of God through Christ."* When God sends the Spirit of His Son into our heart, what then takes place is told by God through the prophet in *Ezekiel 36:26, "A new heart also will I give you, and a new spirit will I put within you: and I will take away the stony heart out of your flesh, and I will give you an heart of flesh. (27) And I will put my Spirit within you..."* This is the mystery of the gospel that the Apostle Paul stated in *Colossians 1:27, "...Which is Christ in you, the hope of glory."*

The above discussion and Scriptures show that there are several critical teachings from God that we must be accepted and received to "faith" before we must make the final decision and step of faith to pray and invite Christ into our heart for salvation. As God taught us about, sin, Jesus, what we should do, we grew in measures of faith; and then we actually did what God required: we humbled ourselves, asked forgiveness and invited Christ into our hearts. God then responded by changing our heart and putting His Spirit, Christ, in us. So, every Christian has THE MEASURE OF FAITH FOR SALVATION. That does not mean that we all had the same measure of faith at salvation, but whatever measure of faith we had at salvation, if God determined it to be enough for Him to respond and save us, then that was our required measure of faith.

ALL MEN HAVE NOT FAITH

Many big name preachers on television and radio programs teach that all people are born with faith, and that for salvation a person must just make the choice to "place their faith" in Jesus. Faith is not a substance, object or anything that a person can just take out and place here and there. They are incorrectly using the word faith instead of confidence or trust which are based on our evaluations of relationships. We can place our confidence or trust in people or things which will fail. Faith will not fail because it comes from hearing God's Word, Christ. Faith is the word which tells that we have accepted God's Living Word, Christ, into our heart for whatever God is speaking to us. The Spirit of Faith mentioned by the Apostle Paul in *2 Corinthians 4:13, "We having the same Spirit of Faith, ..."* is the Spirit of the Living Words God is speaking to you at the time, Christ. The "Word of Faith" that the Apostle Paul mentions in Romans 10:8 is the Word God is speaking or manifesting to you through the Living Word. The Word of Faith becomes our confession-of-faith after we choose to accept God's Word or message to us. It is not a confession we make up; our confession-of-faith is the "Word of Faith" which God gives us.

Babies are not born with faith and then grow up able to place their faith here or there of their choosing. Faith only comes from a willful knowledgeable choice to receive God's Word, Christ, into our heart when the Living Word is revealed to us.

In Romans Chapter 12, the Apostle Paul is teaching on the gifts of the Spirit. He starts out in Verse 1 addressing the teaching to "Brethren" which clearly refers to Christians and we have seen that all Christians have a measure of faith. In Verse 3 the Apostle Paul is telling us to think soberly of ourselves according to the measure of faith we have received from our accepting God's Living Word because he knows that we all have received at least the measure of faith for salvation, *Romans 12:3, "For I say, through the grace given unto me, to every man that is among you, not to think of himself more highly than he ought to think; but to think soberly, according as God hath dealt to every man the measure of faith."*

It is easy to see now that only Christians have faith because faith only comes from acceptance and obedience to God's Word, but there are Scriptures which state that all people do not have faith. God used the word faith first when talking about the children of Israel in *Deuteronomy 32:20, "And He said, 'I will hide my face from then, I will see what their end shall be: for they are a very forward generation, children in whom is not faith."* Jesus also rebuked the disciples in *Mark 4:40* when He said, *"And He said unto them, 'Why are ye so fearful? How is it that ye have no faith?"* Even good people accepting and obeying God in some areas can lack acceptance and obedience to faith in other areas or circumstances. The Apostle Paul who wrote *Romans 12:3 and stated that "...God hath dealt to every man the measure of faith"* states in *2 Thessalonians 3:1-2, "Finally, brethren, pray for us...(2) And that we may be delivered from unreasonable and wicked men: for all men have not faith."* Paul is not contradicting what he said in Romans 12:3. The Apostle Paul was talking about Christians in Romans 12:3, and in 2 Thessalonians 3:1-2 Paul is talking about evil, ungodly people who have rejected God's Words to unbelief and have no faith.

All Christians have some measure of faith; Non-Christians have no faith unless they are responding positively in God's teaching process to bring them to Christ.

NOT ALL PEOPLE ARE CHILDREN OF GOD

The Apostle Paul states in *Romans 8:9, "...Now if any man have not the Spirit of Christ, he is none of His."* And in *Galatians 3:26, "For ye are all the children of God by faith in Christ Jesus."* From the discussion before on measures of faith for salvation, it is plain to see that people must hear and learn from God to obtain salvation: Christ in their hearts because Christ is God's Living Word. Many people totally reject Jesus Christ. Only those people who have received the Spirit of Christ into their heart are children of God.

The fact that people have not accepted Jesus Christ as savior does not mean that God does not love them. God loves everyone with a perfect Love.

God loves us so much as sinners that He sent His Son to die for us to implement the new covenant with mankind. Jesus loved us so much as sinners that He fought the battle of sin and became our perfect sinless sacrifice so we can be set free of our sin debt.

Everyone is God's loving creation, but only those who have received His Son's Spirit, Christ, into their heart are His children.

FAITH DOES NOT COME FROM HEARING, AND HEARING AND HEARING!

Faith comes from accepting and obeying God's spoken Living Word to us. Each time God speaks to us, we must at that time make the choice to accept to faith or reject to unbelief. A person may reject, and reject, and reject, and then finally accept God's Word to faith, but that certainly is not the desired procedure. The stories of the Old Testament show that God very rarely spoke twice or more to anyone that had heard clearly and understood His Word the first time. God spoke to the young boy Samuel more than one time in 1 Samuel Chapter 3. He spoke to Gideon twice in Judges Chapter 6, but these were people who did not understand clearly God's first Word to them, and they were still in doubt. When people understood the first time that it was His Word, God just expected them to trust Him enough to accept, obey and do it.

Some faith teachers teach that because the Words of God or Jesus are "carrying power," or potential faith, that each time we hear God's Words, some of the faith and power in the Words rub off on us as it goes through our consciousness. God' Living Word, Christ, is the Creator who created all things: the heavens, people and all creatures. God's Word is all powerful, but it does not rub off on us as it passes through us from hearing, and hearing and hearing His Word. We must make the choice to faith or unbelief each time we hear God's Word. Also, God's Word does not "carry power:" God's Word, Christ, is power, *1 Corinthians 1:24, "… Christ the power of God, and the wisdom of God"!*

GOD RESPECTS HIS WORD, NOT PEOPLE!

In Psalms 138:2 God's Word states, "I will worship toward thy holy temple, and praise thy name for thy lovingkindness and for thy truth: for thou hast magnified thy Word above all thy names." And the Scripture states in *Proverbs 30:5-6, "Every Word of God is pure: He is a shield unto them that put their trust in Him. (6) Add thou not unto His Words, lest He reprove thee, and thou be found a liar."* God's Pure Word is Christ, but if we change it any, it is not Christ. So, when we change God's Word and confess it, there is no power in what we have said to back up our words, and we will be found a liar. Jesus says that in the last day we will be judged by the Words He has spoken, *John 12:48, "He that rejecteth me, and receiveth not my Words, hath one that will judgeth him: the Word that I have spoken, (Christ), the same shall judge him in the last day."* In Romans 14:12 and 1 Corinthians 3:11-15, the Scriptures state that we will all answer at the Judgment Seat of Christ for the good and bad we have done in the body here on earth. Some of the effects of rejecting God's Word begins instantly in our lives because anytime we reject God's Word we are choosing unbelief instead of faith and are willfully giving satan the advantage in our lives. Ephesians 4:26-27 and 2 Corinthians 2:10-11 state that if we do not forgive others and hang on to anger, we will be giving place and advantage to the devil in our lives.

God does not respect people, but He respects His Word. This causes some people to seem to be abundantly or much more blessed than others. If we want to be in line for more of God's blessings, we must receive more of God's Word to faith which comes from our acceptance and obedience to His Word. Jesus says in *John 15:7, "If you abide in me, and my Words abide in you, ye shall ask what ye will, and it shall be done unto you."* Jesus' Words abiding in us is the result of us choosing to accept and receive His Words into our hearts by faith. As we receive more of God's Word to faith in our hearts, we should at the same time be receiving more answers to prayer. If we are not receiving more answers to prayer, we should seek God and examine our selves to see if we are truly receiving God's Pure Word or not.

The Scriptures in the Old and New Testaments tell us that God is not a respecter of persons. The Scriptures state in *2 Chronicles 19:7, "...for there is not iniquity with the Lord our God, nor respect of persons, nor taking of gifts,"* and in Acts 10:34 the Apostle Peter states, *"...Of a truth I perceive that God is no respecter of persons,"* and the Apostle Paul states in *Romans 2:10-11 and Ephesians 6:9, "for there is no respect of persons with God," and,"...neither is there respect of persons with Him."* We are told in James 2:9, *"But if ye have respect to persons, ye commit sin, and are convinced of the law as transgressors."* This is so good! Because when we read the stories of the Bible and see how God has blessed someone, we can potentially expect the same kind of blessings. For example: In 2 Kings 20:1-11, God sent the prophet Isaiah to tell King Hezekiah to set his house in order that he was fixing to die. *King Hezekiah prayed a simple almost boastful prayer, "I beseech thee, O Lord, remember now how I have walked before thee in truth and with a perfect heart, and have done that which is good in thy sight."* God sent the prophet back to tell Hezekiah that he was going to live and God would give him fifteen more years. Now, since God is not a respecter of persons, all of those Scriptures in Proverbs and Psalms that state if we set our love on God and obey His Word, then He will give us long life are not just good principles to live by, but are true promises. If Hezekiah talked to God about his death and God heard and answered him, then we can too! All of the "special" people of the Old and New Testaments had to fulfill their special callings of service by accepting and obeying God's Word, Christ, to faith, just as we must too.

      Since God exalts His Word, if we "hang" on to God's Word, by accepting and obeying His Word, we will be exalted along with His Word. It is like hanging on to the rope attached to a large helium balloon as more helium is pumped into it. At some time there will be enough lift from the helium to sweep you off your feet and carry you away into the sky. We have victory over and are lifted above this sinful world controlled by the devil when we hang on to God's Word through faith, acceptance and obedience to God's Word, *1John 5:4, "...And this is the victory that overcometh the world, even our faith."* Also, true faith, acceptance and obedience to God's Pure Word will quench all the fiery darts of the devil when he tries to "pop our balloon" and shoot us down, Ephesians 6:16, "Above all, taking the shield of faith, wherewith ye shall be able to quench all the fiery darts of the wicked." Notice it says ALL the fiery darts! The true faith based on the Pure Word will not allow any darts to get through to you. The shield of faith is similar to the promise in *Psalms 34:7 which states,*

CHOOSE FAITH AND GRACE
CHOOSE FAITH - GOD RESPECTS HIS WORD, NOT PEOPLE!

"The angel of the Lord encampeth round about them that fear Him, and delivereth them." I guess we would have to fear God enough to accept and obey His Word to faith for these two verses to be equivalent.

It is possible that we could hear, accept and obey God's Word while dragging our feet, complaining or for other personal reasons. Even though this might seem like we have faith, it is not faith. Faith only results when we with pure intentions accept and receive God's Pure Word into our heart to faith. God knows our intentions, and He will not send His Living Word, Christ, into our heart if we have incorrect intentions. It would be like the Apostle Paul stated in *Galatians 5:6, "For in Jesus Christ neither circumcision availeth any thing, nor uncircumcision; but faith which worketh by love."* If we hear, accept and obey God's Word with the wrong attitude, then we have failed to receive the Love, Spirit of Christ, of the Words that God spoke to us, and we will be doing whatever we do alone without God's help or blessing. The Apostle Paul states the result of doing things without truly receiving Christ, the Love of the Words, in *1 Corinthians 13:1-3, "Though I speak with the tongues of men and of angels, and have not charity(love), I am become as sounding brass, or a tinkling cymbal. (2) And though I have the gift of prophecy, and understand all mysteries, and all knowledge; and though I have all faith(accepted and obeyed God's Word), so that I could remove mountains, and have not charity (love), I am nothing. And though I bestow all my goods to feed the poor, and though I give my body to be burned, and have not charity(love), it profiteth me nothing."* So what do we do if we do not want to do what God is asking of us? There is no sense in doing it with the wrong attitude, so we must pray for God to change our attitude or help us change our attitude so we can continue to be in God's Will and perform what He desires of us. We must admit we do not want to do it, for He knows anyway! Then we turn to Him because we know that whatever He has asked us to do will be better for us, our family and our friends; also, we know He will give us the strength and ability to perform whatever He has asked. The Apostle Paul found out he could do all things through Christ, the all powerful Creator, as he states in *Philippians 4:13, "I can do all things through Christ who strengtheneth me."* We must make sure that we have received the Love of the Words when we go "for the Lord" so that we are also going "with the Lord" or that He is going with or before us.

CHOOSE FAITH AND GRACE
CHOOSE FAITH - GOD RESPECTS HIS WORD, NOT PEOPLE!

It is possible for us to hear and mentally accept God's Word with good intentions of doing His Word but never getting around to actually obeying personally. We give to missions for someone else to go. We pay the preacher and other staff to visit in the hospitals. We contribute to prison ministries to make sure someone goes and witnesses to the inmates. We pay taxes to make sure, or hope to make sure, that the poor are fed. We take our old clothes to the church for the clothes closet. We never personally go to the front line of the spiritual battlefield: we are always at the R(rest) and R(relaxation) camp talking to the returning spiritual fighters. We hear and accept that someone should go do these things, but not us personally. I have met elderly people who when they start reading their Bible more as they think of death, begin to doubt their salvation as they realize that they have never done most of the things Jesus asked us to do; they only gave their money to the church and attended the services and socials.

In the Book of James, James talks about hearing and not doing. We can think we have faith because we hear God's Word and know it is true, every Word of it! But then deceive ourselves by not receiving it personally into our hearts to obedience, *James 2:14, 17, 24 and 26, "What does it profit, my brethren, though a man say he hath faith, and have not works? Can faith save him?(17) Even so faith, if it hath not works, is dead, being alone. (24) Ye see then how that by works a man is justified, and not by faith only. (26) For as the body without the Spirit is dead, so faith without works is dead also."* If we have received the Love or Spirit of God's Word into our heart to teach a class, we will teach the class and with the right attitude. If we have received to faith the Love or Spirit of God's Word to us, we will follow through with any works that God has asked of us. If we do not follow through to complete the actions required, it is not called faith, but unbelief for rejecting part of God's Word.

If we have doubts about our past, whether we really got saved or not, and whether we are truly walking by faith or not, we should not start being upset and worried; we can work it out with the Lord now because He is only a prayer away. We should put seeking God at the top of our-to-do list until we know for sure we have received Christ in our hearts and that He created a new heart in us at salvation.

...AND GRACE

One Sunday morning on a beautiful beach in the Caribbean while sitting with a US Congressman on one side, a US Senator on the other and a margarita in one hand, the devil answers his cell phone with the other hand to take a live report from one of his demons. "Hey boss! Everything is great! Dr. Stanley, Dr. Kennedy, Dr. Duplantis, Dr. Hagee, Dr. Shuller, Dr. Price, Kenneth Copeland, Richard Roberts, Andrew Wommack and 15,000 other preachers across the United States started their sermons this morning with 'Grace is God's unmerited favor!'" The devil was so excited he jumped up shouting for joy, spilling his drink all over the Congressman. The shocked Senator shouts, "What in the world are you shouting about?" The devil replies, "When my word is put first or above God's Word, their messages will not hurt me at all or benefit the people because God only backs up and confirms His Pure Word of truth." Jesus said in *John 14:6, "I am the way, the truth and the life ...,"* in John 17:17 says God's Word is truth and in Psalms 138:2 God has exalted His Pure Word above all His names. When anyone says that grace is God's unmerited favor, the statement is totally untrue, creates confusion and is straight from the devil because *Proverbs 30:5 says that," Every Word of God is Pure."*

All of the ministers mentioned above and thousands of others, who have been living off God's Word and charitable contributions for most of their lives, should all know that "unmerited" is a characteristic of grace but not a defining word for grace. "Unmerited" could be correctly used to describe favor, since it is possible that favor can be earned or "merited." For example, an employee can earn favor by doing a good job. To use "unmerited" as a defining word for grace would imply that there are two graces, merited and unmerited. "Unmerited" is a general characteristic of grace, mercy, compassion and all forms of God's love because we, mankind, do not deserve or merit any of God's love; therefore, "unmerited" is not a specific word to distinguish grace from any other form or manifestation of God's love.

For example, "unmerited" is not a defining word specific to grace any more than "vehicle" is a defining word specific to define the automobile you drive. It is true you drive a "vehicle," but that does not specify whether it is a truck, car, tractor, motorcycle or road grader. "Vehicle" is common to all drivable motorized machines just like "unmerited" is common to all of God's love.

Also, it is totally incorrect to use "favor" to define or describe grace! All theologians and ministers, whether they are trained in Hebrew and Greek or not, should know from a simple use of a concordance that every time the word grace was used in the Old Testament Scriptures, it was incorrectly interpreted and should have been replaced in all cases favor or mercy. Dr. Hagee, from San Antonia, TX, teaches on national and worldwide TV that anyone who believes there was no grace in the Old Testament is scripturally illiterate. The Psalmist says there was no grace in the Old Testament in *Psalms 25:10, "All the paths of the Lord are mercy and truth unto such as keep His covenant and His testimonies."* All the Old Testament people had was God's Love, mercy to them, and God's Word, Truth, to guide them. The Apostle John agrees in *John 1:17 where he states, "For the law was given by Moses, but grace and truth came by Jesus Christ."* Grace is a New Testament word describing the New Covenant relationship between God and mankind! These are simple truths that should be like grade school facts to the thousands of doctors of theology and ministers across our country, yet they are not!

Stating that grace is "God's unmerited favor" is totally incorrect, and only creates or adds confusion which is from the devil who rejoices and benefits when ministers use his lie. Grace is the word we use to describe the actions and changes that are worked in our hearts and lives when the resurrection Spirit of Christ is invited and enters our hearts at salvation, *Ephesians 2:8, " For by Grace are ye saved through faith;…"*. We continue to grow in grace by accepting more of God's Word into our hearts through faith in our walk with the Lord, *Romans 5:2, "By whom also we have access by faith into this grace wherein we stand, and rejoice in hope of the glory of God."* Grace always follows our acceptance of God's Word to faith because when we receive God's Living Words, Christ, into our hearts by faith, the same Living Words, Christ, begins the work of grace in our heart to produce the purpose of the Words God spoke to us that we received by faith. We call any work of the Spirit of Christ

CHOOSE FAITH AND GRACE

in our hearts a work of grace; therefore, when the Spirit of Faith, Christ, enters our heart, we quit calling "it" faith and refer to the following work of the Spirit in our hearts as a work of grace. The Spirit of Grace, God's Living Word, Christ, would not be in our hearts if we had not chosen God's Words to faith by accepting and receiving in our hearts by faith the Words God spoke to us.

The best description of grace, the actions of the Spirit and changes the Spirit makes in our hearts when we receive the Spirit of Christ into our hearts at salvation, is spoken through the prophet by God in *Ezekiel 36:26-27, "A new heart also will I give you, and a new Spirit will I put within you: and I will take away the stony heart out of your flesh, and I will give you an heart of flesh. (27) And I will put my Spirit within you..."* When the Spirit of Christ performs these works in our hearts, we become a child of God and a new creature as stated in *2 Corinthians 5:17, " Therefore, if any man be in Christ, he is a new creature: old things are passed away; behold all things are become new."* It is easy to see that drastic changes take place in our hearts when Christ comes in and adopts us into the family of God, *Galatians 4:6-7states, "And because ye are sons, God hath sent forth the Spirit of His Son into your hearts, crying, Abba, Father. (7) Wherefore thou art no more a servant, but a son; and if a son, then an heir of God through Christ."* The dividing point from being a non-Christian to becoming a Christian is when the Spirit of Christ enters our hearts as stated in *Romans 8:9, "...Now if any man have not the Spirit of Christ, he is none of His."* The work of grace for the changed heart and adoption into the family of God at salvation is the essence of the New Covenant; the Old Testament people received forgiveness when they asked for forgiveness and offered their sacrifices, but they did not receive the Spirit of Christ in their hearts and become children of God. In *1 John 1:9 the Scripture states, "If we confess our sins, He is faithful and just to forgive us our sins, and to cleanse us from all unrighteousness."* The Old Testament people only received forgiveness and a covering for their sins; we get forgiveness and cleansing in our hearts from the sins along with becoming children of God.

Many people today would want to become children of God if the importance of faith and grace, and their relationship, were explained simply and clearly by ministers who were really concerned for their listeners' salvation rather than just filling their part of a program or show. People's eternity is at stake, and this is why it is especially critical that ministers teaching God's Word should be careful to show respect for God's Pure Word and not slight the Spirit of Grace by teaching careless errors when the truth is so great! When anyone states that grace is "God's unmerited favor" they are creating confusion and speaking despite, insult and scorn, unto God's true and wonderful Spirit of Grace, as stated in *Hebrews 10:29, "Of how much sorer punishment, suppose ye, shall he be thought worthy, who hath trodden underfoot the Son of God, and hath counted the blood of the covenant, wherewith he was sanctified, an unholy thing, and hath done despite unto the Spirit of grace?"* The Spirit of grace is a special manifestation of the Holy Spirit in our hearts, and it is a very serious situation or condition to willfully speak against the Holy Spirit.

CONCLUSION

     I am so grateful that God in His mercy spared me through the twenty four years I thought I was a Christian and was not. My life had become so bad in my heart that when Christ did come in, I recognized several fantastic changes immediately: love instead of hate in my heart, changed desires about money and other physical things, a love for God's Word, a love for people and a strong desire for everyone to receive Christ into their hearts so they would not have to go to hell and Lake of Fire because of the devil's deceptive lies.

     During those twenty four years that I only thought I was a Christian, I suffered and caused others to suffer much hurt and heartbreak because of the deception of the devil, and I still continue to reap some hurt from those years of sowing even today. Everyone should know of the great grace and changed heart God has to offer to any person who will call on Him in truth. It is so sad the true simple gospel of the changed heart is not being preached clearly across our country; if it were, many more people would turn to God through Christ because everyone who is not a Christian is trying right now to fill a void in their hearts that only Christ can fill. Even when ministers do preach about the changed heart there is so much error in their messages about faith and grace being God's unmerited favor that very little benefit comes from the messages even though they may sound great and make people feel good. Therefore, the true pure gospel, or Word of God, is not being preached across our nation or around the world correctly. The present conflicting, powerless interpretations of Scriptures cause confusion among Christians and non-Christians alike across our nation which hinders God being able to work like He wants to through His people. We all need to get several different copies of the Bible with a concordance as we research and seek the truth of God's Pure Word if we care for ourselves, our families and our nation. We cannot continue to wait for and expect our spiritual leaders to tell us the truth, for they have only been taught how to explain the Bible according to the beliefs of their group or denomination which in many cases is not the true, Pure Word of God. There are a lot of smart, dedicated, sincere, moral people in every denomination, but they obviously cannot all be correct and many must be teaching errors since some teach the exact opposite of others. Jesus points out that many people will think their condition with God is correct but tragically find out too late that it is not, and then they will perish without an opportunity to correct their error. Jesus explains in *Matthew 7:22-23, "Many will say to me in that day, Lord, Lord, have we not prophesied in thy name? And in thy name have cast out devils? And in thy name done many wonderful works? (23) And then will I profess unto them, I never knew you: depart from me, ye that work iniquity."*

Each of us will stand before God at the Judgment Seat of Christ individually, and then what others believe or have taught will not be an acceptable reason for our personal lack of knowledge and understanding. We each are personally responsible for our relationship with God, so we must not depend on others any longer! If we honestly seek God, He will teach us His Word. You might be blessed by being in the "perfect church," but if you are not personally seeking God, it will not help you one bit when you stand before God. When we become a Christian, it is our responsibility to study to grow in Christ, faith and grace, to become the "priest" reaching out to minister to those we meet daily in our personal world. Regardless of how others believe and serve God, our relationship with God is still our own personal responsibility.

Now I ask, "Do we love ourselves, our family and our nation enough that we would be willing to make some necessary personal changes, even in our beliefs, as we see the true Scriptural meanings of some of the words discussed before: faith, grace, hope, trust, belief and sin?" There will not be a great outpouring of God's Spirit for revival in our nation unless we each decide to let Him change us! We personally have the choice of what we want God to do in our nation, but it must start with us! God does not just pour out revival. He has been encouraging revival ever since Adam sinned by sending prophets, priests and even His Son Jesus to draw mankind back to Him. He only responds to us even as Christians when we individually invite Him into our hearts to make changes. The choices are between each of us and God, so what will your response be? Are you willing to humble yourself and let God make changes, even in your beliefs if necessary, or shall things continue in the direction they

CHOOSE FAITH AND GRACE
CONCLUSION

are going to an anti-God, anti-Christ society? Saul, in Acts, Chapter 9, changed from the ignorant unbelief of persecuting Christians, which he thought was God's will, to actually becoming the Apostle Paul, one of the greatest Christians, because when he was faced with the truth, he accepted it and changed his belief. Whether we are in willful or ignorant unbelief like Paul, Jesus is hindered from doing miracles in Christians' lives today and in our society as He was hindered at His hometown in *Matthew 13:58, "And He did not many mighty works there because of their unbelief."* Cornelius and Peter humbled themselves and changed to God's "new way" for Jews and Gentiles to relate to each other in Acts, Chapter 10. Pride is the only thing that will stop us from repenting and turning from any willful unbelief or changing from ignorant unbelief when it is exposed by the truth.

If every Christian would commit to allowing God to work in us to bring about the changes He wants in our hearts and lives, God would start working miracles in our nation so great that the non-Christians would see or hear what He is doing and want to be a part of it. I do not know what will be down the road for us, but if we will all seek the Lord together it will be a lot better than the path our nation is on now. Let's join together and become the people God can use as faithful Ambassadors to teach His Pure Word and watch Him change our nation: it will be exciting to see what He does!

Books By The Author

"Choosing Faith with Love"
see a summary at www.rahardin.com.

"God Loved Esau"
see summary at www.createspace.com/3448063

"Prayer Changes Things"
see summary at www.createspace.com/3453781

"Choose Faith and Grace"
see summary at www.createspace.com/3465162

"Mercy, Grace, Charity"
see summary at www.createspace.com/3482157

"Jesus"
see summary at www.createspace.com/3482215

Weekly Radio Program

"Choosing Faith with Love"
www.ktlr.com
Click on "Listen Now" in top right corner
Every Saturday Morning
9:30-10:30 a.m. Central Standard Time
in the Oklahoma City Local Area
KTLR – AM 890 on the dial, or FM94.1

NOTES

NOTES